Mark Tyrrell

NEW WAYS
OF SEEING

The art of therapeutic reframing: How to use your
words to release your clients from limiting beliefs,
including examples from 81 real cases.

Contact the author: http://www.unk.com/blog
First Edition 2014
© Uncommon Knowledge 2014

ISBN: 1902892267
ISBN: 978-1902892269

Acknowledgements

I'd like to thank all the clients who have enabled my colleagues and me to exercise and improve our therapeutic creativity.

Mark Tyrrell

Table of Contents

INTRODUCTION
The art of the reframe

~⌒~

There is nothing either good or bad
but thinking makes it so.
—WILLIAM SHAKESPEARE

On a wet afternoon back in 1993 I sat at the top of a run-down old building waiting for my first paying client. I was a newly qualified psychotherapist, specialising in hypnotherapy. I was extremely nervous. As I sat in trepidation in my consulting room on the third floor of the Victorian health centre, I could hear him coming slowly up the creaky stairs towards my room. I had no idea what problem he was bringing with him. Perhaps he had been traumatised by some awful experience? Perhaps he was clinically depressed? Or a survivor of terrible childhood abuses? And what would he be like? Maybe someone was pressuring him to come and he would be cynical about therapy, sceptical, and wary of me. My imagination was still toying with me, whipping up my nerves still further, when he finally entered the room. A tiny, elderly man, he beamed at me, and we shook hands. Then, very politely, he asked, "Do you think you could help me relax while playing the piano?"

Since helping that charming old piano player, I have worked with countless people young and old, from a wide variety of backgrounds. I've helped clients so badly traumatised they couldn't close their eyes without seeing vivid reenactments of various horrors. I've seen people with phobias of all sorts of things: belly buttons, wrapping paper, corners, beards, bin liners, and storms, as well as the more common spider, vomit, snake, height, dental, and flying phobias. In the course of my work training health professionals in clinical hypnosis and psychotherapeutic practice, many of these clients were successfully treated in front of students. Through the years I've helped cancer patients with pain control and worked with the suicidal and depressed, the brokenhearted, survivors of kidnap and attempted murder, people hearing voices, the socially anxious, professionals who feel like frauds in their work, the disappointed who need direction, the chronically angry, and the—seemingly—hopelessly addicted. In fact, I often feel as if a great caravan of humanity has passed through my therapy room. Thankfully, I have usually been able to help, but I have also benefited from what that human caravan taught me.

Shaking 'reality'

Working with so many different cases, as well as giving me more confidence, has made me appreciate one of the most powerful therapeutic tools available to us—the re-frame. Of course, you need many skills and a great deal of knowledge to be an effective therapist, but an apposite reframe of a client's situation or viewpoint can provide the all-important catalyst for change. In fact, sometimes it can be *all* that is needed to tip the first domino and trigger his or her own latent momentum for change. Effective therapists will always release rigidity and reintroduce flexibility of thought within their clients, but time and again I have noticed how quickly people experience a 'eureka' moment once a powerful reframe has shaken and broadened their view of reality. Harnessing this power, and using it to maximum effect, is what this book is about.

How does it work?

Rigid perspectives

When we are highly emotionally aroused (overly anxious, angry, frightened, depressed, etc), our thinking becomes the all-or-nothing, black-or-white variety. Such simplistic, polarised thinking makes it difficult, or even impossible, to see the wider picture. A pertinent reframe (or carefully chosen metaphor containing a reframe) can jolt us out of this 'trance' and help us to see, for example, that our situation *won't* last forever, that it might easily be due to other causes than what we had supposed, and that we *do* have other options.

Likewise, when someone is stuck in a particular thinking style and unconsciously assumes that their (limited, negative) view is the *only* perspective, then a major shift can occur when another wider, more flexible, and positive view is unexpectedly and unarguably demonstrated to them. After such a reframe moment, it is usually impossible for them to maintain the problem behaviour in the same old limiting way. This is similar to how humour and jokes show us another aspect of reality: we think we know where a line of thought/joke is going, only to be unexpectedly presented with another frame of reference, or 'pattern', which sheds a totally different light on things. And once this frame has been perceived, it is always available to us.

Whether we realise it or not, we always assign meaning to things that happen to us, classifying and interpreting events as 'good' or 'helpful', 'bad' or 'worrying'. It is useful to remember that it is *human perception* that makes these value judgements. Without us perceiving it as such, an earthquake is neither bad nor frightening; it is just an unobserved and valueless event. However, although these frames of reference help us to make sense of the world, they can also lead us into a limited and restricting way of thinking. Some might empower us ("I am fundamentally a determined and intelligent person"), but others disempower us ("I'm timid, afraid, weak, and stupid"; "Other people are always out for what they can get"; etc). Again, sensitively given, a suitable reframe can help people to question the value judgements they have made. But simply reframing someone's situation directly back to them ("You haven't got a job, *yet*"), although it offers hope, isn't likely to be enough to shift their perspective entirely, as we will see.

Vital ingredients

It's tempting to try to 'correct' what you see as a self-defeating frame of reference as soon as you spot it, but, as with many things, timing and approach are crucial. You also need to have developed good rapport with the person first (this can be done quite quickly and is an essential skill in effective therapy). However, even with good rapport, there are still things to avoid. For instance, trying to change someone's mind through reasoned argument is unlikely to work because even well-intentioned direct contradiction of a person's beliefs or experience will always break rapport to some degree. If someone stubs his toe and is in pain, then telling him that he feels comfortable will conflict with his experience so sharply that he'll feel completely misunderstood by you.

Likewise, simply telling someone that she is bright or attractive, if she *sincerely* believes with her whole being that she is *not*, will fail. You might spot that someone holds a self-limiting belief, but it is vital to remember that this is *his or her* belief and thus must be respected rather than trampled on. As we are more than aware nowadays, beliefs are powerful; some people are even prepared to die for theirs. Glibly confronting them head-on breaks rapport by conveying the message: "What you think is *wrong*. You should see things *my* way." This makes you appear dictatorial or confrontational. So, how *do* we start to chip away at the tyranny of negative restricted belief systems, while still maintaining rapport?

A subtle, indirect approach is called for. For instance, innocent questions or observations (such as "I'm just thinking aloud here…") incorporating misunderstandings or truisms, while apparently making small talk, can render the information far more likely to be taken on board. It helps to normalise clients' situations—"Oh right, you've got a vomiting phobia. I help lots of clients with that." This will quickly reframe their experiences as nothing much out of the ordinary and offer hope to people who, by the time they come to see you, may well be convinced they are 'completely mad', past help, and totally different from everyone else. (Other ways of presenting reframes include metaphors, storytelling, and jokes, as we will discover in a moment.)

This is the beauty of incorporating reframes and metaphors into the therapeutic work you do: they can be slipped quite naturally into conversation with clients. By the time they come for therapy, most people are genuinely desperate to change and are therefore very likely to pick up on them—like life belts thrown to the drowning. This is especially true if you deliberately pay attention to the types of metaphors and language styles they *themselves* use, and then subtly employ similar language and imagery in your reframes and metaphors. This not only enhances rapport, but also bestows the reframes and metaphors with greater significance for your clients. However, because we can never predict *exactly* what will hit home, or provide that penny-dropping moment, I also apply the 'scatter approach', throwing as many different reframes and helpful metaphors as I can into the general therapeutic mix of a session to see what sticks.

Using direct reframes

Although directly contradicting someone's viewpoint or experience can prove problematic, direct reframes can be helpful in some cases, if sensitively handled. In some circumstances, responding to someone who announces, "I have reached the bottom and can sink no lower!" with, "Well, then, the only way is up!" might be just the jolt he or she needs. But we do have to be careful judges of when such an overtly direct approach is appropriate.

It is often a good idea, therefore, when using direct reframes, to subtly acknowledge the client's original frame of reference in some way before expanding on it or presenting a new perspective. This in itself can provide an opportunity to slip in a subtle reframe. For example, if a client declares, "I can't go on living!", the therapist can respond with, "Of course you can't go on living *the way you've been living your life until now.* We need to look at making changes." This acknowledges what the client has said and even seems to agree with it (and an essential component of rapport building is, of course, that people need to feel heard), but adds a new positive, reframed twist; the client's viewpoint is immediately put into a new perspective *relative* to his or her former way of life, rather than remaining an absolute, hard-and-fast reality.

Likewise, someone might say, "I hate it when it rains!" You could reframe the meaning of his or her statement as follows: "I know, it can be a pain, but if it *never* rained, the planet would die, no crops would grow, and we'd run out of water. And no doubt we'd soon stop enjoying the fine weather, because we always take for granted what is constant." And so on.

Or you might hear a client declare, "I am a *total* failure!" You could point out (in a nonconfrontational way) that 'failure' is a relative term, and then direct his attention to areas in which you know he has been successful. For example, he might have been married for a long time, which many would see as a tremendous achievement. This would mean that he has lots of skills and resources that he might not be consciously aware of at that precise moment, but which you can draw his attention to. You could also mention that failure can be a vital part of the preliminary journey towards 'success', and so forth.

Conscious reframes like these, carefully used, can have a powerful effect, especially if they are given by someone in authority or by someone the recipient admires or respects. But they can also be problematic, and it is well worth being aware of the drawbacks.

As I have mentioned, if you try to overtly counteract or contradict a client's frame of reference too soon, it will break rapport because it will make him feel misunderstood. By initially agreeing with his frame of reference, or at least those parts you *can* agree with, you can maintain rapport and then slip in a reframe later, when he is less alert to any possible 'threats' to his limiting view. If a client declares, for instance, that "I have reached the bottom; I can sink no lower!", you could, instead of the more bullish "Well, then, the only way is up!", reply with, "I can see how it must feel like that at the moment." This conveys agreement, but also includes an important ray of hope. 'At the moment' implies, perhaps for the first time in the client's experience, that his predicament is temporary (which, of course, it is). Although only a very subtle reframe of his situation at this stage, it is one that isn't likely to be contradicted or resisted, and you can build on it.

But there is another reason direct reframes might not work. More often than not, you won't be the first person to have attempted to consciously reframe your client's situation for them, and yet they are still 'stuck'. This is because people who are deeply entrenched in a negative mind-set will automatically dismiss or filter out direct reframes because they contradict their negative view of life. So they may perfectly, genuinely express that "You would say that, because you're my therapist", or "Yeah, I *know* you're right, but it doesn't make me *feel* any better!" Although they might recognise the truth of what you say with their 'thinking' brain, it has no real effect on their 'emotional' brain and therefore on how they perceive or react to the situation. This is where the more subtle use of metaphorical reframes comes into its own.

Metaphorical reframes

Because the mind works to a large extent through metaphor and pattern matching, metaphorical communication is intrinsic to us all. We are fundamentally metaphorical in the way that we think, act, and communicate; we talk, dream, and even sing in metaphor. All language is, in fact, a stand-in for reality. The word *chair* is, of course, not itself a chair but a verbal symbol, a metaphorical representation of a chair. And our conversation is peppered with analogies. When we liken one thing to another—"that sandwich tasted like cardboard"—we take one pattern that fits another to broaden our knowledge and increase our understanding of the world. For a person to absorb a new frame of reference, therefore, a new pattern needs to be presented. A metaphor can act as a new pattern that mirrors the pattern of someone's circumstances or frame of reference in some way, but also has a hopeful element or a 'solution' pattern contained within it. By communicating the beneficial pattern in this way, we avoid its possible rejection by a person's more analytical side.

Someone who is feeling hopeless about his panic attacks, for example, may find it helpful to be given the analogy that his overactive fight-or-flight response is like a faulty car alarm that, instead of going off on the rare occasions it's genuinely needed, has become so sensitive that it keeps being set off unnecessarily. We need the car alarm to alert us when someone is trying to break into the car, but it needs to be (and *can* be) reset so that it doesn't go off every time the car is rocked by the wind.

This panic-attack/car-alarm analogy, therefore, presents the panic attack as a *useful* response, rather than a sign of going crazy, but still a response that needs to be reset so that it only goes off under the right circumstances. It thus reframes both the anxious feelings and the client's perceived helplessness. His panic is now presented as a tool or a function (albeit one that is currently misfiring) rather than an 'illness', and the more hopeful idea that the inappropriate panic can stop happening is subtly introduced by talking about resetting the car alarm to be less sensitive. This is a very different, and far more helpful, way of communicating to someone about his or her panic than merely saying, "There's nothing wrong with you, really. We can do something about it."

When we present a pattern in the form of a metaphor or analogy like this, rather than spelling things out, we are also leaving it to the person to make the connection himself, whether at that precise moment or later. Sometimes the 'a-ha!' moment that enables him to absorb the different way of seeing and experiencing his situation is a conscious one; sometimes it is unconscious. Whichever it may be, it is far more powerful and more likely to change his behaviour when he makes the connection himself.

Metaphorical reframes are ideal for dropping into the general conversation of a therapy session. When a client announces, "I have reached rock bottom; I can sink no lower. There's no hope for me!", you might, as we have seen, initially agree with him: "I can see how it must totally feel like that at the moment." But then, later in the session, after having discussed all kinds of other things, or even *after* the session when the therapy has apparently ended, you can come back to counter his viewpoint, perhaps with something along these lines:

> Oh, yes, I love children's curiosity too…You know, I was reading a story to a child the other day, about a hot air balloon. He was fascinated to find out that hot air rises and that something so still and inert as an enormous hot air balloon could actually *lift up* majestically into the air. And as we continued the story he was captivated by the idea that everything that had been hidden—the wonders and beauty of the surrounding landscape—would suddenly come into view as you *start to rise up*. Although he really hadn't thought it possible before that a great big balloon, stuck right down in the bottom of a

rocky valley, could ever begin to *lift out of that place*, with help and a little guidance, he found to his joy that it did…

Now the pattern—that something that seems 'stuck in the rocky valley' can rise up again—might seem a pretty obvious match to the client's feeling that he has reached rock bottom and that there is no hope. But by presenting this idea much later in the session, the match won't seem so obvious. This reduces the likelihood of it being consciously picked up and rejected. Of course, the metaphorical reframe needs to follow on smoothly from what you have moved on to chat about (perhaps, in this case, children). In this way we can smuggle in a therapeutic reframe and see if it fits, just like Cinderella's slipper.

The pattern of not believing something to be possible, but then finding it happening anyway, echoes one part of the client's predicament: that he believes there is no hope of 'rising up' above his own situation. But if his unconscious mind picks up the new, more positive pattern and metaphorically runs with it, it will provide a powerful reframe of his situation as not necessarily permanent after all, however 'stuck' he might feel.

Tailoring metaphorical reframes

Tailoring metaphorical reframes like this—by listening out for the type of metaphors the clients themselves use, and then using similar language and metaphors yourself—makes them more meaningful to your clients and increases rapport. One man who loved soccer talked about his work 'goals', about wanting to 'be a team player', and how he didn't know what to 'aim for' anymore. His therapist was easily able to adapt these metaphors when working therapeutically with him. Similarly, if someone has a particular interest in computers, it's easy to devise analogies and metaphors that reflect this, talking in terms of 'updating programs in the mind', for example. Creating appropriate metaphors inspired by clients themselves is a powerful way of working, but it is also useful to collect a canon of generic stories to use for a variety of problem states.

For instance, when working with someone who has suffered terrible abuse early in life and who feels inferior because of his or her experiences, I will sometimes tell that person the Native American version of the Cinderella story.[1] In this version a young woman is neglected by her elderly father and bullied, tormented, and scarred with cinders from the fire by her two older, proud, and attractive sisters. She is made to clean and cook and do all their bidding. But it is the neglected and abused young woman, and *only she*, who can see what others can't: the unity of the trees and the stars and the lake, and how they all connect to her destiny. Because she can see what others cannot, and because she has no false pride, arrogance, or vanity, she is the only one who can marry the invisible being and claim her true destiny.

It's a beautiful, hypnotic story, and like any story, it can work on different levels. But for our purposes here, we can see how it can act as a wonderful metaphorical reframe. The abused, neglected child grows into a wise and fulfilled woman partly *because of* and not just *in spite of* what she has suffered. Without minimising anyone's suffering, the story indirectly offers a new meaning to the trials of life as a possible vehicle for later fulfilment. Just saying, "Well, maybe your suffering has made you stronger or less conceited than others who haven't been through what you have"—even if this were consciously accepted by the client—wouldn't allow for unconscious processing of the new pattern. As we have seen, it is this *unconscious* pattern matching, prompted by an appropriate, well-delivered metaphor or metaphorical reframe, that produces lasting changes of perspective.

An added advantage of using a story, joke, or metaphor to present new patterns is that if the smuggled reframe is rejected (or doesn't 'stick'), you won't have lost any rapport. All you will have apparently done is told them a nice relaxing story, a harmless joke, or an interesting metaphor. But in fact, we tend *not* to reject metaphorical ideas, because it's not clear what there is to reject.

In short, metaphorical reframes are wonderful ways of bypassing the more analytical part of a person and presenting alternative viewpoints or solutions to the part of the brain that matches patterns to situations and therefore decides (unconsciously) what our reaction to the situation should be. They are a useful, nonthreatening way to present more positive and appropriate patterns, which the client can match immediately or some time in the future.

Reframes can be demonstrated

Experiences can also work as reframes. If you remove a phobia[2], for example, as well as having a new experience and subsequent memory (a new pattern) of *not* being afraid of whatever the object of the phobia was, you will have helped to reframe the *perception* of it too. An awful lot of therapy is actually about reframing people's experiences of life, as numerous examples in this book will show.

Thus events or actions can reframe fixed ideas or viewpoints as effectively (and sometimes more so) as pertinent, well-timed words. For example, a therapist might give a task to a client that, if carried out, will act as a powerful reframe. I once gave a young woman who was terrified of being humiliated by tripping up in the street the task of *purposely* falling over in public. Successfully reframing the experience for her—from something she feared dreadfully, to something she couldn't bring herself to do, to something that she *could* do, but that annoyed her because no one had actually paid any attention—succeeded in ridding her of her constant anxiety. After that experience, she could never feel the same way about the possibility of tripping up in the street again.

Emotional glue

Successful therapy has more to do with *feeling* differently than just thinking differently. So a reframe needs to have an emotional impact as well as an intellectual one. It is a myth that thought comes before emotion, and that to change our emotional responses to things, all we need to do is change our thinking. Emotional responses actually *precede* thought.[3] The emotional impact of any reframe, therefore (whether the emotional response is laughter, surprise, or even shock, confusion, or hope), is the glue that will stick the newly presented frame in place. After all, emotions are what spur us on to do things in life.

As many of the case studies in this book demonstrate, successful reframes often work on an unconscious level—and metaphors even more so, as they present new patterns to the unconscious mind. Our rational, conscious minds can reject or argue against anything, but once a new, broader, and more flexible pattern has been presented and absorbed below the level of conscious awareness, no argument is needed to get people to discard their damaging, limiting beliefs. One of the best ways of implanting a reframe, and helping clients rehearse and embed new desired behaviours in their imagination, is to use deep hypnotic trance. Hypnosis is a way of artificially accessing the REM state, the brain's natural learning and programming state[4], and as such is a very powerful tool for therapy.

The aim of this book

When people come to us with psychological difficulties, it is usually because they are stuck—their current way of doing things isn't working—and in addition to our therapeutic skills, they need, in effect, to 'borrow' our brains and objectivity for a bit. After many years' experience in psychotherapeutic practice, I am now both confident and realistic enough to know that although I can't 'cure' everyone, most people can be helped to some degree—especially if their readiness to change coincides with the right combination of timing, focus, and input from me.

Over the years, I have learnt that the best therapy happens when we see people as they *really are*, rather than how *theory tells us they should be*. One of my aims in writing this book has been to share some of what I've learnt as I've endeavoured to be the best possible therapist I can be.

It is important to work creatively, but also to practise therapy from the perspective of current psychological, sociological, and biological understandings—rather than from unsupported theory—keeping an open 'beginner's mind' (free from prior assumption) and always remaining strategic and solution-focussed. There are, of course, clear steps to doing effective therapy (which we won't go into here), but having thoroughly absorbed these and incorporated them into my practice, I now often find that when I sit down with someone, it feels more like an art than a science. Relaxing and allowing my own unconscious mind to produce creative interventions produces results that sometimes surprise me, but that often prove more than apt. This book aims to share with you some of the really creative moments that my colleagues and I have experienced in our work with many different clients.

A word of caution: the examples given here are *not* stock panaceas you can apply to anyone regardless of individual differences and circumstances. If some of the examples fit your clients' particular experiences or situations, then that's great, but always bear in mind that you need to tailor therapy specifically to the individual you are working with. The reframes, metaphors, and analogies cited in this book were not the *only* approaches used to help those clients; they were always part of and in addition to a wider strategy—additions, nevertheless, that frequently proved to be significant catalysts for change.

Every example comes from a genuine therapy session, but in every case we have changed personal details to protect confidentiality. They are essentially reframes and 'perspective shakers' designed to loosen up thinking around problem areas and open up possibilities for beneficial change. The practical or 'uncommon' therapist treads carefully around belief systems, ensuring that his or her clients feel understood and connected—even if their beliefs are damaging and restricting. Metaphors and creative reframes allow us to present healthier, less rigid perspectives without conflicting with the client's own view on life.

Much of therapy is about helping people see their behaviour patterns 'from the outside'. This book illustrates this reframing process in action. I hope it will provide you with ideas that you can use and adapt, and I also hope it will inspire you to come up with many creative ideas of your own.

Mark Tyrrell, Brighton, 2014

I publish a free weekly therapy techniques email. If you'd like to receive it, you can sign up here:
http://www.unk.com/blog/free-audio-book

As an extra thank you for buying my book, you'll be able to download the audio version of the book after you've subscribed.

Miscellaneous reframes

A diamond doesn't know its worth

A therapist friend had a client who was particularly frightened in groups of people, and terrified of meeting new people. When she asked the client what it was about meeting new people that he found particularly scary, he replied that he hated the feeling of being judged.

During the subsequent session, the therapist talked about meeting new people in terms of 'connection' and 'merging' rather than 'separateness' and status: "When we meet people, we can—in a way and for a while—partake of and share *their* qualities and attributes; and they can also share ours, so there is a collective 'qualities pool', which can really make a social event!"

This was more effective than trying to argue the client out of his perspective by telling him how successful, interesting, and attractive he was. As we've seen already, the quickest way to break connection with someone is to directly contradict his or her view of reality. Later, the therapist slipped in, almost as an aside: "You know, a diamond doesn't know of its own value and beauty—but it is there nevertheless."

After this interjection she rapidly changed the subject, but the client had heard!

Hands as friends

Sometimes it's useful to assign individual identities to parts of the body so that, for example, a smoker can be encouraged to 'be fair to their lungs' or 'respectful of their ovaries', etc. One worried mother brought her seven-year-old son for therapy because he was incessantly picking the cuticles on his left hand with his right hand. This caused frequent bleeding and was resulting in significant cuticle recession. Having ascertained that there was nothing major currently worrying the boy, and that his behaviour had become a habit, the therapist chatted to him about his life. The boy talked about his school, and so the therapist asked about the other children there and how they got on, and soon it was easy to raise a question about how many of the boys would get into fights. This all helped to build rapport by matching the boy's model of the world. Then, using similar language, the therapist suggested that the boy's two hands could 'begin to get along' and could even 'shake and make up'.

Controlling the control freak

After many years of unhappy marriage, Helen divorced her husband. Always an actively religious man, he had often abused his position in their local church to threaten and control her. She felt very scared of him and the particular church he belonged to, although it hadn't rocked her own faith. But, although her ex-husband had remarried and started a family, she could not be rid of him and his controlling ways. He had made a threat that wherever she moved he would follow and never be more than one hour away. This thought terrified her; she felt she would *always* be controlled by him, even though they were no longer married.

The therapist mused for a while, looking thoughtful, and then actually laughed. She said:

> This is amazing! A man who likes to control so much, a man who likes his power! I'm sorry, but can you imagine it? He's just settled his kids into a new school, his wife's got a new job, he's successful and settled in his own job, and suddenly he's got to up sticks and move again—all because you,

4

on a whim perhaps, decide to move to the other end of the country! He would be entirely at *your* mercy! You could make plans to move, he would then sell up and move, only for you to then decide that you're not going to move after all! Gosh, do you realise how much control over his and his wife's and their children's lives you'd have? In fact, either way, you win! Either you're in total control of *his* life or, which is more likely, he just won't let himself be controlled in that way!

The previously terrified Helen began to laugh herself, and said, "Yes, I know there are areas of the county that he hates! I could move there, or plan to. He wouldn't know whether he was coming or going—I can do my work anywhere, but he can't!"

In this case the therapist just *saw the pattern* of control and realised who really held all the cards. A perfect reframe may just be an accurate perception of how things really are. This is why an effective therapist will be able to remain objective and see the bigger patterns, not getting too drawn into detail.

When strong means weak

A young woman, Tina, was desperate to find a partner with whom she could build a meaningful, long-term relationship. The problem was that, in her attempts to meet the right man, she had got into a pattern of going to night-clubs, flirting, picking up men that she found attractive, and then sleeping with them. As she was really looking for a far more emotionally intimate relationship, she was finding these one-off experiences unsatisfying and unfulfilling, and she was becoming depressed and frustrated about the situation. She admitted to me that the men she found attractive were always tough and silent types—in her words, 'strong men who can't show their emotions'. To which I replied that in my belief, 'strength' implies the capacity to *do* something, not to be *unable* to do it. This shift was quite a shock to Tina, who eventually learned that there were many types of strength that could be attractive.

Different trees

Sometimes, after abusive or difficult childhoods, people can feel like 'damaged goods'. Yet research shows that adverse conditions in childhood can, for some, actually increase adult hardiness and resilience. Knowing this, I will sometimes start chatting with such clients about the differences between various types of trees.

> Have you noticed how you get those 'spoilt' little trees that just grow straight up in overprotective plastic cones, but then you'll see a great oak tree, full of character, that has grown up standing alone in the middle of a field or a park, having survived thunderstorms and maybe even lightning strikes, winter snows, torrential downpours, and scorching summers? Trees like that grow up beautiful and interesting, full of character, with different aspects and wonderful angles to them, and they can do and be so much! They provide shelter, shade, and safety for squirrels and birds, as well as the small plants and flowers that are attracted to them and grow up by their roots. Children enjoy climbing in their rambling branches and people admire

their natural magnificence and grace as they wander past. Yet each tree, which survived through so much, grew from just a tiny acorn.

And then I'll swiftly move on to something else, so that the analogy can be absorbed but not overanalysed.

When ahead means behind

A young, semiprofessional racing driver who was cutting his teeth racing go-carts but had the aspiration and ability to race at Formula One level, went to see a therapist for help with an unusual problem. Despite doing incredibly well—he was winning every race he entered—whenever he took the lead in front of the other drivers, he would find that he actually felt far less comfortable than when he was positioned just behind the leaders. He complained that when he was out in front he would become incredibly nervous, and begin to focus on the people behind him and what *they* were doing instead of concentrating on his own driving. The therapist told him, "In truth, you are *always* behind!" This stunned the young man, who couldn't think what on earth the therapist could be talking about. The therapist continued, "You are *always* chasing something: time! Forget what's happening behind you, and you can fix your attention instead on chasing the time in front of you, so you can get quicker and quicker, trying to improve your personal best, race after race."

Reluctant exercise

Some people are reluctant to exercise, and for a number this may be because they focus on the hard work of the experience of exercising itself, rather than on how good they feel *after* they have exercised. Many people who over-eat do something similar, albeit with the opposite emphasis, when they think about food and eating. As they anticipate eating something, their focus will be on the few pleasurable moments spent eating rather than the hours of guilt, regret, indigestion, etc, that will inevitably follow. When working with such clients, it is useful to drop in reframes to help refocus their attention on the benefits of their desired changed behaviour. With someone reluctant to exercise, for example, we might talk about how all the hard work involved in organizing and packing for a holiday is soon forgotten when the benefits are enjoyed. And, of course, daytime exercise gives your body a great reason to sleep well at night.

The bigger picture

Focusing on one small part of an experience—whether it's the marital row at the end of an otherwise delightful evening or the slightly crooked nose on an otherwise symmetrical face—can spoil one's appreciation of the whole. People who say, "The evening was ruined!" because part of it didn't go so well, or who feel that they are 'ugly' or 'hideous' because their teeth aren't exactly as they would like them, are not working with the bigger picture.

It has been said that generally women tend to notice detail more than men do. And certainly many women will say things like "I don't like my ankles" or "I hate the gap in my teeth." Men, however, are more likely to generalise their perception and get a sense of the whole physical image rather than letting detail and specifics spoil their appreciation.

At the extreme end of the tendency to let attention to specific details spoil the bigger vision, we find body dysmorphic disorder. With this disorder, the sufferer believes that something very specific, such as the dark circles under her eyes, is making her appear totally hideous. Often the supposed imperfection is not even noticed by others, but for the sufferer it feels real enough to blight her life.

A young woman called Rachael came to me for help, as she was feeling very down and lonely. She was attractive, but her mother had told me before our meeting that one of her problems was that she was obsessed with the belief that her lips were too thin and that no amount of lip gloss seemed to make her happy with her appearance. She was very worried that her daughter would go for some potentially dangerous surgery that she really didn't need. Rachael certainly seemed attractive enough to me, and her lips looked even and quite full, but I knew better than to try to *argue* her out of her fixation. So I tried another tack:

> **Rachael:** I don't go out anymore because I know people will see my lips and realise how ugly I am...
>
> **Me:** What kind of evidence do you have that they are looking at your lips and think that you're ugly?
>
> **Rachael:** Well, I see them looking.
>
> **Me**: Do you like that picture? [*pointing to a painting on the wall*]
>
> **Rachael:** Yes, it's very beautiful.
>
> **Me**: OK. Can you move over towards it and get right up close to the painting? That's it. Now stand

right up against it with your eyes just inches away. What do you think of the picture now?

Rachael: Well, obviously it's just a smudge. It doesn't really look like anything. It's just a bit of colour.

Me: Is it beautiful?

Rachael: I can't say it's beautiful. Looking at it this way.

Me: OK, now walk back again…What's happened to that nonbeautiful smudge now?

Rachael: Well, now that I'm seeing the whole picture, the smudge doesn't really figure…

Me: That's right. When we see beauty, we see the overall effect, not the detail.

Later on in the session, as Rachael relaxed deeply in a hypnotic trance, I suggested she visualise various beautiful landscapes and then get up close to examine specific details in each, and to notice how the smaller elements within each landscape didn't always contain anything nearly like the beauty of the whole. At other times, we talked about the books she particularly liked, and I asked her to bring a favourite book to one session, which she did. I asked her to open the 'lovely book' at random and tell me the first word she saw, which was 'the'. I then asked her if that single word was 'lovely'. A few weeks into therapy, Rachael started going out again, and on her own admission, and to her mother's delight, she stopped thinking nearly so much about her 'imperfect' lips.

Swinging vines

Creating a vivid image in the mind that parallels a person's situation is a powerful way to help him or her to see a new perspective on it. Brian, a middle-aged man, had been trying for some time to cut down the number of sleeping pills he took each night. He wanted to go from 25mg back down to 10mg, before eventually coming off them altogether. I asked him what was different when he was taking less medication. He said that before a particular family bereavement, he had been doing meditation every morning, and half an hour of yoga before breakfast. I suggested that we focus on getting him back to this healthy routine. Later in the session, as he was deeply relaxed after I had induced hypnosis, I presented the following to him:

> And, you know Brian, something can *seem* to be supportive and even *look* supportive, but in actuality it doesn't really support you in the way it might seem to. And we could imagine a monkey swinging through the forest and selecting a vine for a while that looks more like string, and even feels like string, and actually it isn't that sturdy or

healthy...and what a relief it is when the monkey leaves that behind and selects a healthy, strong supportive vine.

This idea matched the pattern of his situation. He had been using a system of support (the sleeping pills) that wasn't *really* supportive or healthy, but was now something he could begin to leave behind as he selected a healthier support (the 'healthy vine') to take him into the future. I suggested, too, that from now on the monkey could only instinctively select the truly healthy and strong vines to support itself on its journey through the trees.

Later in the session, I also put forward the idea that his healthy way of life (the daily meditation and yoga) was a pattern that was always there for him and that all he had to do was 'join it'. This may seem strange, but if I could get him to feel that all he had to do was join something that was in some way 'already there', Brian would feel more motivated than he would if he felt he had to start something new himself from scratch. Remember, we were dealing with the way he *felt* about starting these new healthy behavioural patterns, not what he *thought* about them. I said, "You know those merry-go-rounds we all went on as a kid? Imagine you're on one now, and it's spinning around...It has its own momentum, and all you have to do is jump onto it at just the right point, and then you too *take on that momentum.*"

After this session he did indeed manage to wean himself off the medication and was able to 'jump' back onto his healthy lifestyle.

Scary assertiveness

For some, the thought of having to be assertive has become a frightening concept. So one therapist I know tends to talk about assertiveness with his clients in terms of 'giving honest feedback' and 'fair relationship management'. This reframe is especially useful for people who value honesty.

Dispassionate love

A woman in her early thirties came to see me because she was struggling to get over the end of a relationship. She and her ex-boyfriend worked in the same office, so she had no choice but to carry on seeing him every day. This was reopening the wound almost continually, stopping her from grieving properly and moving on. To help the healing process, she really wanted to feel more detached when she saw him. So as we chatted I spoke to her about the 'different sides to love' and about how we don't just stop loving someone in an instant, but the nature of our love can change from passionate to dispassionate, and so we can still love someone, but in a different way. Then, when she was nice and relaxed, I got her to imagine him 'acting cold' towards her at work while she herself felt detached and relaxed. She found she was able to imagine this very clearly. Thus, by *experiencing* relaxed 'dispassionate love', she could still see him at work but without it causing her so much upset or denying the way she had felt for him.

The mind as a calm pool

Most of us have noticed how, when we are highly emotionally aroused—for example, when we are extremely angry—it is difficult to see the wider picture, the other person's point of view. This is because emotions evolved to prompt us to action, and so we need to narrow down our options so we can decide what to do. We can see this with the flight-or-fight response: Do we flee from the big bear in front of us, or do we stand and fight it? However, the downside of this is that *any* strong emotion (anxiety, depression, fear, etc) will narrow our focus of attention and limit our perception of the possible options available to us. Strong emotion distorts how we see our lives and stops us from seeing the bigger picture. And the more emotional we become, the more distorted our perception and thoughts. To communicate this to people, I'll often liken the mind to a pool of water. When it is stormy and agitated, its reflection of reality becomes fragmented and distorted. Once the surface of water is calm, however, its reflection of reality becomes much more accurate and even. Life decisions and strategies are much better if they come from such times of calm reflection.

The importance of secrets

For many clients, it's not just their own feelings and problems that they have to worry about; sometimes there may be great added pressure on the individual from his or her family, colleagues, and/or friends to get better. This in itself can cause tremendous extra strain that they patently could do without. A colleague of mine sometimes helps to take the pressure off her clients by talking about 'secret health'. She suggested to one client that she should keep her new status as a nonsmoker secret, and let other people find out for themselves her new state of health. Secrets are powerful things!

'Spitting out' criticism

Sometimes clients will have been overly criticised in the past and have thoroughly 'digested' the criticism. In other words, they have 'swallowed' it so that it has become part of their identity. Of course, the person who was (or is) doing the criticising may well have some fair points. But if, in the main, the criticism consists of negative overgeneralisations, then it will be of limited 'nutritional value', and may even be counterproductive to someone who is already emotionally distressed. These were the terms I used about criticism when working with Penny, a newly qualified teacher whose confidence was being severely dented by the continuous criticism she was receiving from an older colleague. I explained to her that we could decide whether we wanted to own criticisms or not. I also spoke of the choice between swallowing a criticism and just 'chewing it over for a while' before deciding you don't like it—and then spitting it out.

Feeding by not eating

When working with Stewart, a young male anorexic, I would describe his avoidance of eating as *feeding the anorexia*. This not only introduced a valuable reframe of his condition, but also used language that encouraged him to see his personal identity as totally separate from the anorexia. For many clients, simply viewing their depression, anorexia, addiction, or whatever it may be as something *separate* from themselves that is trying to cheat or control them, can be very liberating and give them a totally different outlook on their situation. The condition is not *them*, not an integral part of their personality that they have to learn to live with, but something outside their core identity that can therefore be tackled and overcome. As I continued the session with Stewart, I spoke about 'starving out the parasitical anorexia by eating'. In this way, 'eating' became 'starving' and 'starving' became 'feeding'. Any idea or metaphor that loosens the rigid perceptions and thinking patterns necessary to keep a condition in place can be a useful way to help escape its grip.

Standing up to anger ✓

Similarly, when working with a man who came to see me with serious anger issues, I separated the anger from his core identity in the language and metaphors I used. I said, "You can be *ready* for that anger next time, and put it in its place by letting it know who's boss!"

If we see a condition or emotional disorder as fundamentally separate from who we are as a person, then it becomes easier to free ourselves of it.

24

When bullying is just a try-on ✳

How we label things strongly affects people's perceptions of what is happening to them. Both his parents and teachers had told young Simon, repeatedly, that he was being bullied at school. His parents, however, became concerned that although he had dealt with the teasing and bullying quite effectively in the past, he was now beginning to worry about it, and was not keen to go to school anymore. The therapist soon realised that although Simon had previously had plenty of confidence, and the resources with which to deal with the taunting he was getting, the 'bullying' label applied by the adults around him was making him worry about it and see himself as a powerless victim. The therapist began (and suggested to the parents that they do likewise) to talk about these teasing times in terms of "When people try it on with you!" This language limits the behaviour to specific times, making it feel less pervasive, and also frames it as people *trying*, and therefore not necessarily *succeeding*, to do something. After chatting for a while like this to the therapist, Simon felt better about learning ways of dealing with other children's attempts at 'trying it on' than he had felt about the thought of standing up to bullying.

25

Waste of Space

When people genuinely feel they are 'a waste of space' or haven't achieved anything, it is often because their highly emotional state is simplifying their thinking, so that they overgeneralise and catastrophise about their situation. This causes them to focus on and magnify negative aspects of their lives and ignore their achievements and skills.

In such circumstances, instead of arguing with them and risking breaking rapport, we can reframe 'space' as 'potential'. One young woman, an Oxford university student who appeared highly talented in many areas, was nevertheless genuinely convinced that she hadn't achieved anything, was a waste of space, and was therefore totally undeserving of being treated well by other people. Musing out loud, her therapist suggested that perhaps people can be treated respectfully because of things they are *going* to do in the future—their potential value (it might be argued that being a student is valued because of the *potential* benefit to society). Later in the session the therapist developed a metaphor about a patch of ground that was "seemingly inactive ground that may appear to be a 'waste of space'

26

but that, in fact, is rich with nutrients and has been sown with countless seeds that even now are growing under the ground, and will burst through the soil at some point in the future".

Time to close the account?

Some people find it difficult to be assertive within relationships. For whatever reason, they may feel that they should put up with whatever is dished out to them by the other person. With clients in such a position, it is often useful to look at what 'a relationship' actually means. If we take the concept out of its personal and emotional context and view it from a much less emotional one, then people will often 'see the pattern from the outside' and develop a new frame of reference around it.

Julie, a middle-aged lady, often found she was being manipulated and frequently found it difficult to set boundaries for herself. So during our first session I talked to her about the nature of relationships:

> You know, a relationship always needs to be based on reciprocation, giving and receiving, rather than manipulation or status. Even kings and queens need to give something to their people in return for the privileges they receive—otherwise there is no real relationship, just a dictatorship or tyranny!

Likewise, you have a relationship with your bank, but in order to continue to have that 'relationship', you need to give as well as take. If you continually take from your bank without putting anything back in, they will eventually close your account, because as far as the bank is concerned, no proper relationship exists at all!

Of course, we also need to help people (and not simply in order to receive something in return), but if you are receiving nothing at all in return, then you need to think about how much of an overdraft you are prepared to allow, and when it's time for you to think about losing that account.

In our next session, Julie reported that she had found this idea an extremely useful one for 'setting limits' and 're-viewing people's accounts'.

Misapplied competitiveness

Linda, a high achiever in her chosen career, booked an appointment for help with confidence issues. Although doing well at work, she vividly described to me how uncomfortable and nervous she always felt whenever she was in the presence of someone she deemed to be better than her in some way—whether they were prettier in her estimation, or cleverer, or paid more, or whatever. So I said to her, "You know, you are a very competitive person, and in many ways that's a good thing, because it has taken you far in life…But any tool, and I mean absolutely *any* tool, can be misapplied and overused…What you call your troubling occasional lack of social confidence could easily be described as 'misapplied competitiveness'."

For this woman, this was an entirely fresh way of viewing her feelings in such situations, and it helped her begin to lose the overly black-and-white perspectives she had been applying.

Womanhood ✳

Anna came to see me looking worn, ill, and extremely upset. She was twenty-seven and had been suffering from anorexia for about twelve years. Although she had been hospitalised many times, she felt that the condition had only ever been contained, never satisfactorily treated, and she was desperate to be free of it.

She sat now in my therapy room, painfully thin and obviously scared. On the one hand, she knew what she was doing to herself was damaging, and yet she couldn't stop feeling frightened and disgusted by the idea of being 'fat and ugly'. I spoke to Anna at length about her life and her hopes. She told me that she was distraught that her menstrual periods had stopped again and said, "You know, Mark, I've never told anyone this before, but I would really like to have children someday."

I worked long and hard with Anna, but very early on, I also started doing something that, looking back, I think made a big impact. I stopped talking about the anorexia or even eating disorders and always referred, instead, to her improved eating habits as *reclaiming your womanhood.*

Bit by bit, Anna began to relax more around food and began to see eating as reclaiming what was rightfully hers: her femininity. She, too, began to refer to times of healthy eating as 'reclaiming my womanhood'.

One day I noticed her skin looked better and her eyes sparkled. "You look like a real woman," I told her. She beamed back at me: "I've started my periods again and do think I am looking more curvaceous." Talking in terms of her femininity, rather than being fat, overweight, or thin, had allowed her, through time, to reframe her situation from that of 'starving herself away from fatness' to 'starving herself away from her birthright' (another term I repeatedly used throughout her therapy). Now she herself was talking about 'curvaceousness' and 'womanhood', which was a clear sign that my simple reframe had taken in her mind.

When someone has had lots of treatment that hasn't really worked, try describing her problem to her in different terms, reframing it back to her. Remember, this doesn't mean saying to someone, "Why don't you think about it like this..." because that can very easily break rapport and seem dictatorial or confrontational. Instead, simply adjust the way *you* refer to her situation. This can help subtly reorganise her own thinking around the problem and shift her towards positive change.

Anna sent me a lovely card a few years later telling me she was married and expecting a child. She was, she said, loving and enjoying her birthright.

Using what your client values

If someone you are working with obviously places great value on particular traits, such as loyalty and friendship, then you can make beneficial use of this in your therapeutic work. Admired qualities such as these can be transferred onto the problem situation to make potential solutions seem like more positive, attractive, and motivating examples for a client to follow.

When Ken called me up for an appointment, he sounded depressed and looked as much when we subsequently met. He stared vacantly into the middle distance, had trouble focussing, and complained of 'feeling tired all the time'. We talked about his life at the time, about the primal human needs we all need to meet to live fulfilling, satisfying lives—such as security, connection to others, autonomy, and a sense of meaning. We found various areas of Ken's life that needed work and focussed on those areas.

While working with Ken, I couldn't help but notice the automatic negative spin he'd put on events. We worked on this too. And, to help keep his stress levels down, I taught him some simple relaxation techniques so that he could relax deeply and regularly. He soon looked visibly more refreshed and relaxed, and he began sleeping better again.

But during this time I also became aware of a specific pattern. Whenever anyone scoffed at, or was dismissive of, activities that Ken really enjoyed or was interested in, he lost confidence in those activities. This had happened time and time again, with the inevitable result that he now did little that he enjoyed. He needed to 'bat for his own side' and stand by his ideas and interests.

One ex-girlfriend had scoffed at his hobbies of going bird watching and painting watercolours, so he had abandoned these interests too, and never gone back to them since. Something was only 'valid' for him if others thought it so; if not, he simply didn't have the confidence to pursue whatever it was, even though it might bring him great satisfaction and enjoyment.

So, while chatting with him, I decided to drop into our conversation a reframe around his relationship to his interests—and hopefully improve his general self-confidence as a positive side-effect. I already knew that Ken valued loyalty highly as a trait, both in himself and in other people. He'd also said that being a good friend was important to him. So I said, "Those interests and hobbies of yours are like friends that you could be loyal and respectful towards. If others don't see their qualities, you can still stand by your friends [interests] and protect them. You can be true to them and get back in contact with these friends whenever you want to."

Not long after I presented this analogy to him, Ken told me he had decided to do a bit of bird watching again, as 'spring was on its way'. He also took up painting watercolours again and told me, with a conspiratorial smile, that he didn't really care what other people thought about what he liked doing.

Cats do it so well

Being ill with something as serious as cancer brings many trials and tribulations. Treatment can be lengthy, painful, and often uncertain. From time to time the medical professionals will inevitably need to carry out a number of different tests, and waiting for the results of these can be very trying for patients. They may find themselves constantly worrying about the tests, unable to concentrate, perhaps having difficulties sleeping. None of this does their health any good.

If I treat someone with a serious condition such as cancer, I am always mindful not to be disrespectful by offering her platitudes or acting like I know what she is experiencing. Because I don't. Instead, a good way to build bridges is to take the *pattern* of her experience and hold up another pattern that seems to match it in some way.

Melissa, for instance, had been diagnosed with breast cancer and was now awaiting test results to see if the tumours had spread. When she came to see me I was careful not to offer her undue hope, or to tell her that everything would be fine. She was obviously in distress, however, and wanted help with the 'anxious agony of waiting', the horrible uncertainty. So we talked at length about her likes and dislikes, and she spoke glowingly about her cats that she loved. When she was deeply re-laxed and in a hypnotic trance, I offered her the follow-ing analogy:

> You know, Melissa, we don't just have thoughts about things, do we? We also have feelings about them...And I'm sure there have been many times in your life when you have had to deal with, even relax with, uncertainties...And doing that becomes a skill in itself...And all you could do was to say to yourself that, whatever happens, however things turn out, you'll cope somehow... but for now you'll wait...And cats do it so well... When a cat watches a mouse hole, it just relaxes in the moment...It doesn't need to preempt, or to imagine, or do anything at all except wait, and relax with the waiting, without trying to guess what will happen before the mouse emerges, or even trying to guess if the mouse *will* emerge... It just waits and relaxes...comfortably ready for anything that it may need to do...in the future... when the time comes.

Melissa later reported to me that she'd really loved this image of a cat just 'sitting pretty' and waiting. I did three things here with this analogy:

1) Reframed tolerating the uncertainty (even relaxing with it) as a skill that can develop.

2) Linked the learning of this skill to her favourite animals, cats, as she found it easier to learn from a cat rather than from me advising her directly or from reading a self-help book written by someone she didn't know.

3) Linked the contemplation of a pleasant thing for her (cats) with an unpleasant thing (waiting for uncertain test results), thereby giving her a more positive association for the experience she was currently enduring.

Size matters

Nowadays we live in a culture that tends to give a lot of weight to material things and the way we *appear*. And for many of us, such considerations have come to be more important than what we are actually like as a person. We seldom hear about character or personality; our society in general tends to focus on what someone has or looks like.

Kevin came to see me because he was obsessing about his size:

> **Kevin:** It really bothers me that I'm only five feet six inches tall. Whenever I go into a room I feel that other people are judging me, that they'll think I have nothing to contribute.

> **Me:** Gosh, it must be really difficult to feel like that! And do you feel that you have things to contribute?

> **Kevin:** Oh yes! I have lots of ideas for taking projects forward at work. And I know I am actually very driven and creative.

Me: When you enter a room, it is not just your physical self that enters—it is the size of your ideas... And remember, ideas, perceptions, your perspective can grow to an infinite size...You have heard it all before, and I am not going to repeat the fact that Beethoven was five feet four, the same as the hero Lord Nelson, or that the poet and visionary William Blake was a little less than five feet tall... And who now thinks, when they hear Beethoven's Fifth, that the great genius, who continued to compose some of history's greatest music after becoming stone deaf, was five feet four inches tall, or that Alexander the Great was said to be much shorter than the average man of his day? These were in no way small men, and when they entered a room, it was their towering ideas that came with them.

Having chatted to Kevin on the phone previously, I already knew that he felt underconfident about his height, and therefore I had deliberately memorised the short statures of some great and 'large' historical figures. I studiously avoided Napoleon's oft-quoted five-foot-one-inch frame as too cliché, and I enabled myself to talk about other great men's diminutive frames by telling him that I was not going to "repeat the fact that..."; this is a paradoxical way of giving yourself permission to do exactly what you have just said you were not going to do! This stopped him from thinking, "I've heard this before!", which would have shut him off to what I had to say. And because of the way I suddenly reeled off the heights of legendary men, he was so surprised that the reframe had a chance to enter his 'attention gates', as these were pried open by the shock of me having so many exact heights of different men right on the tip of my tongue.

It is also important to point out that I didn't ignore his anxieties around his height; instead I sought to link the concept of stature to *ideas* rather than physicality. Throughout the session I talked in terms of what these great men *did* and asked him about his own big ideas, and I got lots of information about them. He left telling me that he really felt the 'sky was the limit'. And in the next session he reported a newfound confidence when entering rooms and meeting new people.

Taking liberties

Effective anger management is one of the most important emotional skills. Once we can manage anger, we can negotiate, relate, and empathise much better with others, as well as avoid the pitfalls of excessive anger, which include increased risk of heart disease, not to mention social and professional damage. When we become highly angry, the pumping efficiency of the heart drops, often seriously, leading to arterial damage and lowered immune function.

Extreme anger effectively puts us into a trance state: rage narrows our perspective to a pinpoint from which the validity of other people's opinions vanishes. Just like in a dream, you are able to hold quite bizarre, black-and-white opinions that afterwards can seem stupid even to you! But during the 'anger trance', you believe fully in anger's view of things. So, to get control over anger, we need to break this trance before it gets a chance to get going.

Sean was a very angry man. When he decided to seek therapy for help with his apparently uncontrollable anger outbursts, he was under threat of dismissal from his job as a deputy manager in a warehouse because he kept exploding and shouting people down. He would also be very person-ally abusive to work colleagues, which he knew was grossly unprofessional.

> **Sean:** It's just that I don't like being taken for a fool by anyone! If I start to think that someone is taking liberties with me, then that's it. I explode, say what I think, and get myself into trouble and hurt other people.

> **Therapist:** Sean, you are on your final warning at work, right?

> **Sean:** That's right.

> **Therapist:** And you have a young family and a wife at home?

> **Sean:** Yes. That's right.

> **Therapist:** So, how much longer are you going to let that anger make a fool out of you?

> **Sean:** [*laughing*] Well, I suppose it *has* been taking liberties with me, hasn't it?

> **Therapist:** That's right—and I think it's time you stopped letting it push you around.

Here the therapist neatly personified anger as something (or someone) that had been pushing Sean around and 'tak-ing liberties'. Sean had already stated that he couldn't stand people taking him for a fool, so all the therapist did was reframe the anger as something/someone that had been 'making a fool of him'.

By hearing what motivates a person and then associating it with a stance against the problem, we can intensify that person's motivation to change. Thus Sean, who was hyper-vigilant against people who 'might be about to make a fool of him', became hypervigilant against whenever his own anger was about to do likewise. The therapist also taught him to rehearse in his imagination while deeply relaxed, increasing his objectivity and staying calm at times when previously he would have typically become enraged. They also looked at his overall lifestyle and addressed various other stressors, but there was no doubt that this reframe helped motivate Sean enormously.

I can't do that

When Malcolm came to see me, he was rather lacking in confidence. We discussed the many changes he wanted to make, but he always maintained they were impossible. He wanted to learn more computer skills in order to get a better job, for example, and to go out more so that he would eventually meet a woman. And he wanted to develop the confidence to travel alone, as he was sick of going on holiday with his 'immature friends' who he felt held him back. But when I asked him what was stopping him from doing these things, he would always say that these were things he just couldn't do! He used the word *can't* so often that it was very noticeable.

Me: Malcolm, how do you know you *can't* do these things?

Malcolm: I just know I couldn't.

Me: Malcolm, when you were three months old, did you know you'd be able to speak one day?

Malcolm: No.

Me: Did you know, when you were six months old, that one day you'd be able to walk into a bank and sign a cheque, or have a conversation with the manager, or drive a car, or cook a meal, or fly a kite, or do the stock market? Did you know, when you were a one-year-old, that you'd be able to speak French? [*Malcolm was a good French speaker.*] Or put fuel in your car, or use a computer, or get on a bus on your own, or surf? How could you have possibly known these things you were going to do? And if you could have spoken about it or thought about it back then, and thought that you'd *never be able to do any of those things in the future*, what would your present adult self say to the you back then about not believing?

Malcolm: I…er…

Me: Can you stand up?

Malcolm: Of course I can!

Me: How do you know?

Malcolm: Because I just can. I've done it before.

Me: But just supposing you'd *never* done it before! Just supposing that this was the very first time you were about to stand up…You might think you couldn't, right?

Malcolm: Well, maybe…

Now this might seem like a strange way for me to carry on! But I knew trying to argue Malcolm out of his fixed and limiting beliefs, about what he was and wasn't potentially capable of in the future, would just be fruitless. I didn't want him to keep blindly arguing for his limitations, so I didn't once try to get him to see that he could improve his computer skills, go out more socially, maybe meet a woman one day, go on holiday, et cetera. Instead, all I did was present the pattern of a time when he undeniably didn't know he could do something versus the evidence of the present day, when he could evidently do such things. He couldn't forget such a startling demonstration and became much more receptive, with the result that he then did make rapid progress.

Ideas as children

I took a similar approach working with a young female art student called Lucy. She loved her art and was full of creative ideas but had little confidence in them. She would feel crushed if anyone so much as hinted that her ideas maybe weren't so great. During our conversation, I discovered that she was godmother to her best friend's children, so we talked about how important it was to nurture and protect children, championing them until such time as they could 'run on their own' and survive independently. I then began (in and out of hypnotic trance) to reframe her creative, artistic ideas as needing to be nurtured, respected, and taken care of just like young children, until such time as they were robust enough to take care of themselves.

Using a metaphor that she could easily relate to, I changed her frame of reference from a lack of confidence in her ideas to needing to nurture and mother her ideas until they were ready. I also suggested that ideas, once in the world, don't just belong to one person anymore, so she should 'look after them!' This reframe worked for Lucy. She immediately felt less embarrassed about her ideas and more protective of them, because ideas 'take on a life of their own'.

Anxiety

W e feel a little tense for a public presentation, and we perform with gusto; we feel terrified, and performance drains away like water down a plughole. Although a degree of adrenaline due to anxiety can heighten our awareness and improve our performance, if the emotional arousal gets too strong, it will hinder us by distracting our attention from what we are doing to what we are feeling—physically and emotionally.

Anxiety and all its associated sensations—racing heart, perspiration, gasping for breath, nausea, etc—are driven by our imaginations. It *can* be a response to real events, but it can also result from, or be exacerbated by, misuse of the imagination—for example, by worrying about something. Our imagination can directly influence how our body and emotions respond. So, if I am hungry and imagine food, it can produce salivation. Or, if I imagine an embarrassing situation, blood can be diverted into the upper levels of the skin on my face and thus cause me to blush.

One problem with using (or *mis*using) the imagination is that we can inadvertently train ourselves to respond to future events in ways that undermine us. For example, if I imagine the public presentation that I'm giving next week while feeling anxious—i.e., in an emotionally driven trance—I am hypnotically training myself to feel frightened during the *actual* presentation.

However, thinking about feared situations and events in different ways can also dramatically *reduce* anxiety. Something is only frightening if we perceive it to be so. If we can view something we previously feared in a new, less threatening way, it can dramatically reduce our anxiety and help us perform better, whatever the situation.

Anxiety can present in a myriad of ways, from full-blown panic attacks or severe phobias, to blushing, having little confidence in oneself, feeling ashamed, and sexual problems. The following 'perspective shakers' helped turn things around for a variety of anxious clients.

Public speaking: Its not about you!

Confident and smart when he first arrived in my office, Darren now sat nervously in front of me. He had been fine until he started to tell me about the forthcoming public speaking he could not avoid doing, as it was for work. At this point he became highly flustered, and a blush began to spread up his neck towards his face.

During the session, I taught Darren how to relax deeply, and using the hypnotic rewind technique, I helped him change the way he recalled his past experiences of public speaking, so that they no longer made him anxious when he thought about them. Then, when he was still in a deeply relaxed state, I said:

> You know, Darren, it is all about the message, not the messenger. That is what I want you to remember from this session.
>
> You are a conduit, a medium, through which valuable information can travel. If people are more concerned with the colour or texture or shape of the telephone receiver, rather than the important message that it can relay to them, well, then they

are not fit to receive the message anyway! You can be a clear, presentable, and entertaining communicator, but remember: the message is really what it is about.

If I bring you a tray of food when you are hungry, the tray is important, of course—it has a job to do—but you really need to be focussed on the food. The food is what is going to give you nutrition, not the tray.

The analogies of the tray and the telephone receiver clearly represent the notion that a presentation should be about the material being presented and not about the presenter. But by communicating this idea using these inanimate objects metaphorically, and while Darren was in a relaxed state, I could make it both memorable and easy to absorb for his right brain. As he left, I reinforced it by saying, "Remember, you are a tray to serve up something special!" I bumped into him several months later, when he proudly told me that he now enjoys public speaking and looks forward to it with excitement.

The stage is your home

Very often when individuals become afraid of speaking to groups of people, they come for help in making themselves feel more comfortable about it. But actually the focus needs to be away from how *they* are feeling! Like a good host, anyone speaking in public needs to put the audience at *their* ease. So, while helping Alan, a young entrepreneur who was terribly nervous about presenting at a forthcoming conference, I said, "And when you're up there, the stage can be your home; it is *your territory* and your *guests* can be led and influenced by you. You can put them at their ease with your words and demeanour."

Only ever one person

It's true to say that someone speaking to an audience is communicating to a 'collection of minds', but another way of looking at it, which can help put people at ease with the prospect, is that we are only ever really communicating to one person at a time. Even if many people are there, it's a group of *single individual minds* that process and connect with your words. So I say to apprehensive public speakers, "There is only ever one person you are talking to at any given moment. And that is the person who understands you and can make the best use of what you have said."

Audience performance

Speakers often assume that the *entire* onus for the success of the occasion rests upon them. However, it can be helpful to point out that it takes two to tango! When a speech goes down well, it's only *partly* due to the quality of the speech itself. The audience also has 50 percent of the responsibility on a public speaking occasion.

Another client who was feeling the pressure of an upcoming presentation at work was presented with this idea by his therapist: "And your audience has to perform as well; they have to listen, pay attention, ask relevant questions, and use a certain level of intelligence. You and your audience need to work together; it's never just you at all."

Generously displaying your humanity

When we present ourselves to our fellow human beings for scrutiny, we like to feel that we can control the image we present, especially if we tend to be perfectionists! But many people who come to me for help with public speaking are deeply worried that they might appear fallible in some way, perhaps by momentarily forgetting what they were about to say. However, when we present to an audience of some sort, we aren't really doing anything more than we do when chatting with a group friends. It is not a *totally* different activity.

In the course of normal conversation, we all forget what we were saying, stumble over words, and commit other faux pas. No one thinks any the worse of us for it. Of course, a planned presentation should be reasonably polished, but not so polished that we run the risk of breaking normal human rapport with our audience! As with much in life, the important thing is what we focus our attention on.

So, I might say to an anxious perfectionist who fears being mortified in public by succumbing to some normal human behaviour in the middle of a presentation: "People want to see that you are human, and so you can be generous to them by displaying your humanity. It is part of natural communication to sometimes forget what you were going to say. If you do this and *relax with doing this* in front of people, then you will impress them with your confidence and humanity. It's the speakers who are relaxed within themselves that make the best impression, not those who never make a mistake."

Happy Limitations

People sometimes feel that problem behaviours are somehow more permanent and less fragile than improvements
or cures. We can deal with this by talking about 'new and
happy limitations'. I once asked a client who was frightened of public speaking to rate his anxiety on a scale of
one to ten, with one being the most relaxed he could feel,
and ten the most fearful. He rated himself at a ten. Using
the power of expectation, I then 'warned' my client that
once the fear was cured, there might be no going back,
and that "whatever might happen, you may never again be
able to get above a three!"—which would be a comfortable
level, anyway. I went on to talk about my own early fears of
public speaking and mentioned how, after treating myself,
I could now never get above the 'lowered ceiling' of three,
even when I couldn't get the slides to work or the PA system acted up! In this way, I planted the idea of permanent,
new, and healthy learning for the client.

Embarrassment and unconscious behaviours

Social anxiety can come and go quickly, but it can also prove quite disabling for some sufferers. And if we become embarrassed *about* our embarrassment, then the social anxiety will linger longer and become even more stress inducing. Working with anyone suffering from embarrassment like this, as well as teaching him any missing social skills he might need, I will invariably chat to him, again while in a receptive, relaxed state, and say something along the following lines:

> Your conscious mind and your unconscious mind work independently of each other.
>
> Your conscious self is the 'I' that rationalises and thinks sequentially. Your unconscious mind is the part that takes care of your breathing, blood pressure, digestion, immediate emotional reactions, and so forth.
>
> It is, of course, possible to *influence* your unconscious, but you can't be expected to be totally in

control of it one hundred percent of the time. You can *influence* an unruly child, but not control its behaviour absolutely. After all, your unconscious mind has to take its own responsibility; if it 'misbehaves', it isn't the 'fault' of your conscious mind.

This unusual notion can prove very powerful when helping people who become mortified by their own autonomic responses, as in the next example.

The blushing bride

Claire was a confident and outgoing marketing executive, but she was become increasingly anxious about being called on to present to her colleagues at work, as she had always had a tendency, ever since she'd been at school, to blush. Not only this, but she was about to get married, and the fear of blushing on her wedding day was ruining all the fun of the preparations. This is a faithful record of our conversation:

> **Claire:** I really blushed when I gave a talk last week. Although no one said anything, they must have noticed! I'm getting so worried about it, I've even started blushing when I talk to my friends. I'm really scared that I'll blush on my wedding day and spoil everything. I'll feel such an idiot!
>
> **Me:** That's interesting. Do you decide to blush?
>
> **Claire:** Er…no! I can't help it. It just happens.
>
> **Me:** But say you went out for the evening, and your friend was rude to someone there. Would you

take one hundred percent responsibility for that rudeness?

Claire: No, of course not. It wouldn't be *me* being rude, would it? It would be my friend.

Me: That's right, and if I blush when I speak in public, I don't take responsibility for it. I didn't *decide* to blush. It wasn't me, my conscious self, that did that. So I don't take total responsibility. My conscious self shouldn't suffer for what my unconscious self has done.

Claire: That's strange. I have never thought about it that way before.

Me: If you take a group of children out for the day, you have influence over them, to some extent, but you don't have total control, because they have their own minds. If they behave atrociously, are they showing you up or themselves? If I blush, I can actually separate my identity from the part of me (the 'naughty child') that produced the blush and think, "You didn't decide to blush, so don't take total responsibility for it."

Claire: I see what you're getting at...

Me: It's enough that you can start to focus on the part of you that had been doing that; we don't need to have your conscious mind suffering as well.

When we seek to alleviate a problem, we can hypothetically 'split' a person into his or her conscious and unconscious parts. If we are not embarrassed about appearing embarrassed, then at least 50 percent of the problem has already gone. Blushing feeds off embarrassment, but if we can relax *about* blushing, then the blushing is denied its life blood (literally).

I developed this idea of conscious/unconscious responsibility further with Claire in a deeply relaxed state. I suggested she didn't have to care whether she blushed or not, thereby dealing with the fear of the embarrassment. Then I got her to visualise in her imagination a sense of coolness replacing the rising heat she would feel whenever the spotlight was on her. Claire, happily, was not a blushing bride—but she *was* a very happy one.

Feeling like a fraud

Alan, a respected local solicitor who ran his own firm, came to see me because of high anxiety levels. Despite his apparent success, he was plagued by the conviction that he was a fraud waiting to be discovered by his colleagues and clients. As we chatted generally about his life and experience, I normalised his concerns by gently observing that this was a familiar worry and preoccupation for many people I had met, going on to openly wonder why that might be the case:

> After all, all labels and professional titles are essentially made up—from surgeons, psychiatrists, and police officers to a whole range of other professions. And as we are all descended from tree-dwelling primates, and have had labels and titles artificially grafted onto us, it's not surprising that at an instinctive level this all feels quite unreal to us if we think too hard about it. Looking at it that way, we are *all* fakes! But, if we relax with that, we can still be damn good at our jobs. We are all primates from the trees, so carry on with the bluff, but make yours good!

Anxiety as water

Very often what a person is worrying about may need addressing in practical terms; they may need to physically *do* something about a situation to stop the worrying. But some people worry about the very thoughts they are having. They are concerned that they have weird, anxious thoughts and that this is a sign that they are going crazy.

A man came to see me after the 9/11 terrorist attacks in America, saying that he had started panicking every time he heard a plane fly overhead, fearing it would crash into him. Not only was he very anxious about the possibility (as he saw it) of being killed by a crashing plane, but he was also worried that 'having such weird thoughts' meant he must be going crazy. When he was reassured that it is entirely normal to experience stress after the major life events he had recently been through (which included divorce, job loss, and the illness of a child) and that this stress could come out in many different ways, he felt much relieved.

In such cases, we can reassure people that it is their emotional arousal that is driving the thinking and not the other way about, as many people assume.

A young woman who was concerned that she got really anxious over 'silly little things' once came to see me for help. I explained to her that anxiety can sometimes act like water in that it seeks a channel to go down. And it doesn't really matter what the thought is that anxiety carves out for itself to be carried along. Once the anxiety and stress levels subside, then the thinking usually sorts itself out. The *content* of the thoughts, therefore, may not necessarily be what is driving the emotional arousal; they may just be convenient 'clothes' for anxiety to give itself form.

All the Space in the universe

When people experience claustrophobia, they feel trapped by the situation they are in. The feeling they report is of sheer panic: "I can't get out!", or "I couldn't get out if I wanted to!" We can point out to such sufferers that imagination developed in human beings as a tool through which we can transcend the boundaries of time and space. In order to solve problems and invent tools, mankind had to learn to momentarily 'leave' the present time and location.

The vehicle for this time and space travel is the imagination, and through it we can imagine new scenarios and examine possible outcomes. If you sit in a room for four or five hours, then chances are you will 'leave the room' via your imagination for some if not most of the time. This can be done by daydreaming or by being wrapped up in a conversation in which absent people or places or times are explored, or through an absorbing activity such as reading or listening to music. Likewise, when you watch TV you can totally forget about your surroundings. Often when I'm on a long train journey, I can forget about being on the train to an extent because I have infinite time and space within my mind. In this way no one is ever confined to, say, an aeroplane, bus, lift, or train.

Bearing all this in mind, we can reframe space and time for our anxious clients:

> And, you know, when you sleep at night, you travel beyond the mere time or geographical location of your bedroom. You have, within your mind, the space of the entire universe within which to travel. You only return to the confines of your bedroom when you awaken hours later, and only then do you remember where you are! The way to relax in a confined space is to remember *you have all the space of the universe* contained and available to you through your mind, and you can access it at any time.

Virgin wine

So much of what people feel they 'should be' and 'should have done' is conditioned through the media, and through feedback from their family and associates. Although conforming to such social pressures is what makes the world go round, it can get out of proportion. If we feel we don't conform to what we believe to be important, necessary, or desirable benchmarks in our society, then we can feel unnecessarily anxious or become depressed.

Several years ago, a young man of twenty-nine, who had grown up in a very macho culture, came to see me. He had a secret of which he was profoundly ashamed: he was still a virgin. He was painfully worried about it. He felt abnormal and 'behind everybody else'. He was particularly worried that when his new girlfriend found out, as she inevitably would, she would think badly of him. Keen, therefore, to reframe virginity as valuable rather than negative or disadvantageous, I introduced the idea of much sought-after new wines: "And I'd like you to just think for a moment about how the longer that wine is left to mature, and the riper the grapes are when they are crushed, the more valued and special that wine is when it is finally poured from the bottle and drunk. After all that careful preparation, when it is tasted at last, it is truly savoured and appreciated!"

The young man found this analogy very helpful, and in a later session talked jokingly about his girlfriend's privilege at receiving something so 'rare'.

Mouth ulcers and flying

Lots of people come to see me because they are petri-
fied of flying, and many find takeoff and turbulence the
most frightening parts of all. This was the case with Neil,
a young accountant who came to me desperate to get rid
of his severe flying phobia because he was really keen to
go on holiday with his new girlfriend. I used the rewind
technique to remove his phobia, but also dropped a metaphor into our initial conversation to back it up. Quickly
changing the subject from what we *had* been talking about
(a great way of creating instant detachment from worrying thoughts), I mentioned that I had a mouth ulcer and
talked about the common experience of feeling an absolutely huge mouth ulcer with our tongue, only to discover
when we look in the mirror that it's actually not that big at
all! Then, later in the session, I picked up on the idea again
and applied the pattern of overemphasizing a mouth ulcer
to the pattern of overemphasizing the angle of takeoff and
the severity of turbulence: "And, you know, it feels really
steep when you're taking off, but when you're watching a
plane take off from the ground, it doesn't look that steep at
all! Likewise, although it feels very dramatic and incredibly

bumpy when you fly through turbulence, viewed from three hundred, two hundred, or even one hundred metres away, it looks as if the plane is flying along nice and smoothly."

A 'safe place'

When helping another flying phobic to relax, I asked him to describe his 'safe place' (the time or situation in which he felt most safe) to me. He readily described taking his daughter to her weekly piano lessons. This was a time when he could truly switch off and relax, as nobody could call him, pressure him, or make demands. At this I couldn't help laughing, much to his surprise, and said that that was *exactly* why I enjoyed flying! No demands, no calls to field, no responsibility…

Air isn't 'nothing'

Sometimes fearful flyers will talk about being way above the ground and being immensely frightened by the fact that there is 'nothing at all underneath them for miles'. To help reduce their anxiety, we can explore this idea of 'nothing' with them. To one client, who had been a nervous flyer for years and kept talking about the 'miles of nothing' beneath the plane, I said: "You know, many people think of air as 'nothing', but of course it actually behaves in many different ways. Just like water, it is buoyant, it has currents and flows…Planes can glide through it and travel on it in very similar ways to a boat over water."

Depression

~⊙

The World Health Organisation has predicted that by 2020 clinical depression will be the number-one health concern in industrialised nations. Rates of depression are rising all the time, and as many as one in three women, and one in eight men, will become severely depressed at some point in their lives.[5]

As anyone who has suffered serious depression can tell you, the experience is horrible. Symptoms include feeling exhausted, especially in the mornings, disrupted sleep patterns, overdreaming, inability to enjoy or reduced enjoyment in things that normally bring pleasure, difficulty concentrating, anxious worrying, morbid fears, unexplained aches and pains, irritability, and becoming emotional or upset for no particular reason. People don't necessarily experience *all* of these symptoms, and some have different signs, but anyone who is depressed will recognise at least some of them.

Despite the prevailing myths, research has shown that depression is *not* primarily a biological disorder, a 'disease'[6], and as it's one of the most common things therapists are asked to help with, it is important to have a thorough understanding of the real causes and cycle of depression, and of how to break it.[7] When treating depressed individuals, many factors need to be considered, such as lifestyle, history, medication, diet, and relationships. The ideas presented in this section are by no means a complete treatment for depression but provide valuable metaphorical reframes that can be used as a part of wider strategies.

First, some words of warning.

Modern psychology developed well before sophisticated apparatus were invented to actually 'see inside' the brain. Metaphors were freely borrowed from the more established sciences to describe psychological phenomena and the functioning of the mind. During the infancy of Western psychology, for instance, hydraulics were all the rage, and the steam engine was the power that drove them. The metaphor for the mind became to a large extent hydraulic. People were said to be repressing their emotions, or to be in need of letting off steam. These metaphors are current to this day, and people still talk of 'running out of steam', 'letting off steam', and 'releasing pent-up emotion'.

Later, with the invention of the electric lightbulb and the science of electricity, psychology again borrowed from 'real science'. People now talked of 'recharging your batteries' and 'being run-down', or being 'flat' and needing to 'recharge'. After World War II came the computer age. Computers had proved their worth during wartime as code-breaking devices, and a new metaphor for the human mind was born: we now talk of 'processing information', 'retrieving memory', and 'crashing'. Although we now know much more about how our emotions and our brains really work and interact with the body, such metaphors can still be very useful when helping the public—in many ways, when depressed individuals awaken in the morning exhausted, it *is* like they have a flat battery.

It is important to note, however, that not all metaphors are helpful. Some can actually be damaging, limiting a person's thinking and keeping him or her in a negative state of mind. Many people probably don't even realise they are using metaphors when they describe their situation, but it is very useful to notice them yourself. Someone might, for example, talk of 'losing it', the implication being that whatever 'it' is has been *lost forever*. In therapy I might turn such an idea around and talk of finding 'it' again. Or even subtly question whether the 'it' can *really* be lost, thus revealing the metaphor for what it is.

Another example of a misused metaphor is the oft-heard 'having a nervous breakdown'. Cars break down (and washing machines, and computers), but people do not.

Describing something as 'broken'—rather than, for example, exhausted—implies that it has completely malfunctioned. We all need to know when we are using metaphor.

A distorting lens

I sometimes describe depression as a lens, one that bends reality in the same way that a prism bends light, distorting its passage (rather than just reflecting light as a mirror does). This is because, despite appearances to the contrary, anyone who is depressed is actually highly emotionally aroused. High emotional arousal affects how we view the world; it distorts and limits our perception, frequently convincing us that *our* view of reality is the only accurate one. This black-and-white, either/or style of emotional thinking evolved to simplify the choices available to us, in order to aid survival. For example, we need to decide *quickly* whether to fight or flee. But if we get stuck in this simplified thinking style, it can seriously affect our lives. Typical distortions include black-and-white thinking, catastrophising, unrealistic expectations of perfection, morbid guilt, continual self-blame, or blaming others.

It is important, therefore (especially considering that someone who is seriously depressed may see suicide as his or her 'only option'), to help depressed clients to calm down as quickly as possible so that they can see the wider picture of their situation and realise that their model of reality is just that: a model. When the highly stressed, depressed brain calms down enough, the more recently evolved thinking brain—which can perceive the more subtle shades of grey—becomes accessible again. Just as calm water will reflect the reality around it much more accurately and evenly, so too will the human mind. When it is calm, it can think much more clearly and flexibly, and is less prone to all the stirred-up distortions of depression.

The restrictive dogma of the depressive regime

Paul was a professor of politics with a special interest in political history. He was soft-spoken, and he had a mouth that was permanently turned down. He spoke without hope in a monotone. "My life just feels so *useless*. My marriage ended a couple of years ago. Yeah, I've got a PhD and I teach, but I still feel useless," he explained to me at our first session.

It was tempting to try to argue with Paul at this point. To contradict him by telling him how bright he was, reminding him that he had recently restructured a whole department at his college, that he was deeply loved by his children, and that he was an attractive and gifted man. He may well have listened to me, but his depression would have rejected it all. What I needed to do instead was to help him realise how depression distorted reality and in effect lied to him.

So later in the session I introduced a familiar idea to him:

As you know only too well, a repressive regime or dictatorship will only allow propaganda and limited versions of reality that fit with the prevailing ideology and beliefs of the tight regime. Any outside information that would contradict the belief systems of the dictatorship are either dismissed and rejected, or distorted out of all recognition until they fit the prevailing propaganda.

And depression works just the same way—it's a psychological dictatorship. By calming things down, other less rigid, more realistic, and flexible versions of reality can be allowed in; practical problems can be solved and basic needs fulfilled. So, what we want for you, Paul, is a democracy—not a dictatorship!

Talking about 'the depression' as separate from Paul's core identity was crucial. I also knew, of course, that the idea of propaganda and selective information filtering into repressive regimes would resonate with Paul, and by talking about 'psychological dictatorships' I was able to draw his interest and present the idea that his perceptions were biased because of the 'ideology' of depression. He could then readily relate to the idea that ideologies change and that systems can become more open.

Uncaged bird

Jane described herself as 'anxious all the time' and 'unhappy', even though her life was seemingly perfect in many ways. Pretty quickly, the therapist working with her detected a measure of 'learned helplessness': we may learn we are powerless in one situation, and then carry over the *feelings* of helplessness to situations where, in fact, we are *not* helpless.

Throughout her childhood, Jane had lived in various foster homes and felt unhappy much of the time. She had also been in a series of abusive relationships, but had now found a kind and gentle man who treated her well and whom she loved—so much so that they were engaged to be married. But despite all this, and having built up a successful career for herself, she felt terrified that any minute 'something horrible' would happen. Emotionally she was responding as if circumstances hadn't changed for her at all.

Jane's therapist worked with her for several sessions and made many successful interventions that helped her enormously. Towards the end of their time together, however, despite acknowledging that she felt much better than she had at the start, Jane said that she still felt afraid, as if she 'didn't deserve to be happy': "I love my fiancé and my life is good, but sometimes I feel as if I can't go anywhere or do anything, and even that my own money is not mine to spend!"

To which the therapist replied:

> OK, Jane, I'd like you to imagine a young bird that was free for only its first few days of life and then locked up in a cage. This bird is beautiful and has a wonderful song but is never allowed to sing or fly free because the door is always locked. One day, however, through sheer hard work and some luck, it finds the cage door open. Now at last it can fly free. It can sing and fly as much as it likes. But it doesn't. It just stays in the cage. Now, if you could speak to that bird, Jane, what would you say?

To which Jane responded, "Well, I would tell it to fly free, of course…because now it can, only it just doesn't know it!"

This was as far as the metaphor went, and the therapist quickly changed the subject, but within a short while Jane did begin to behave and feel more 'free'. And at the very last session she said, "Thank you so much. I feel I have been released!"

Ending up

Some people project their imaginations into the future and create depressing and lonely scenarios for themselves. This is obviously not a good idea, especially as many then come to believe that this imagined future is *inevitable*. In our therapy practice, we constantly hear clients saying things like: "I see myself *ending up* in one lonely room by myself, with not even a cat for company!" or "I'll end up bankrupt and lose everything!" We can question the whole notion of 'ending up' without directly challenging the client's reality model:

> It's fascinating, isn't it, that there's nothing so certain as change? The seasons change, the weather changes day to day; even when it looks set to rain for hours, the sun can appear from behind a cloud. Fashions change—sometimes we like them, sometimes we don't. And people change too; they can move and learn right up to the point at which they die. And even after death the process of change doesn't stop, as our body itself then goes through many changes.

That last point isn't necessarily something to say to an anxious client, but it's true nevertheless!

Worthy of the gift and being made a fool

Georgina came into therapy feeling very despondent and down about her ongoing divorce. After seven years of marriage she had filed for divorce because of her husband's continual deceit and unfaithfulness. This was her second marriage, and the first had ended for similar reasons. At the start of therapy she was in danger of negatively overgeneralising and accusing *all* men of a lack of trustworthiness, therefore damning all potential future relationships before they had even started. Overgeneralising *specific* negative experiences to cover *all* future and present experiences is a common feature of the emotionally driven thinking style of people who are depressed. But Georgina also felt that there was something about her that made men think 'target'. She felt she had been an idiot to trust her husbands and was scared of being 'made a fool' of again. Part of her therapist's strategy, therefore, was to reframe her current idea of trust:

Georgina: I feel that there must be something about me that attracts men who deceive and cheat.

I have been made a fool of so many times, how can I ever trust again? Even honest men might see something in me that lets them think it's OK to cheat on me!

Therapist: You are a generous woman, Georgina, and you can continue to give generously. When you trust someone, you give them a gift. And you can decide whom you give your gift to, but once you have given your gift, it is up to the receiver of it to protect the gift of trust that now belongs to them. If they fail to maintain this gift or neglect it or break the gift, then that is their doing—a reflection on *them*. Once you've given your gift, you've done *your* bit!

"I want to kill my baby"

A young woman called Sarah, who was still suffering from severe postnatal depression six months after the birth of her first child, came for therapy. She was distraught as she confessed for the first time that she often felt so desperate that she wanted to kill her baby to stop its constant crying and end the nonstop pain she was feeling. She felt like a monster for having such thoughts.

"Well done!" said the therapist.

"What?" replied the young woman, genuinely shocked.

The therapist continued, "Well done for choosing not to! You could easily have done it. You felt desperate enough and had the opportunity, but despite how bad you felt, you *didn't* do it. That shows tremendous strength of willpower. And added to that, you've decided to do something about it—you've come to me for help."

Sarah later said that this one comment had been an absolute revelation for her, and was almost enough in itself to turn her life around again.

New frontiers

We all know that we can't change the past, but sometimes we may need a little help to let it go. Some people talk about being haunted by their past (and of course, traumatic memories do genuinely need to be dealt with), but undue focus on the past can stop us from looking forwards to our future and, in effect, paralyse us.

Jennifer was severely depressed when she came to see me, and we worked together for several months. I helped de-traumatise some awful memories of abuse (using the rewind technique), and we looked at solving current issues and enabling her to challenge her own negative thinking. But I noticed that she was still prone to overfocussing on the past. She had, unfortunately, had years of the type of psychotherapy that encourages past focus, and so now had been trained to be able to do little else. It was clear she still believed that therapy must consist of long trawls through an unchangeable past; yet it was also clear that wallowing in the past like that was making her unhappy, and that to live productively she needed to enjoy her present life and look forward to and plan for her future.

On one occasion when she was again talking wistfully and regretfully about past times, I interrupted her:

Me: Jennifer, can I ask you something?

Jennifer: Certainly!

Me: If you imagine a long, old-fashioned, Wild West wagon train rolling along to new frontiers... where do you suppose the wagon chief would sit?

Jennifer: Well, I suppose they would sit right at the front, because they are leading the train. They need to direct it.

Me: Do they need to be looking back or leaving the wagon train to constantly ride back to survey the landscape they have already covered?

Jennifer: No, they would be going forward. They would need to focus on discovering new frontiers. [*Jennifer was beginning to get the point.*]

Me: I suppose they need to be aware of the landscape they have been through so as to be prepared for any future eventualities, but ultimately they are going someplace new, and need to be looking forward, do they not?

Jennifer: [*laughing*] OK, OK, I've got the point!

By creating this imaginary wagon train and talking of 'new frontiers' (Jennifer's words, not mine), I could present the pattern of needing to focus more on where we were going in the future, while admitting that as long as she had learned from the past, then she could leave those 'landscapes' behind. This is very different from just telling her to forget about the past, because having to make the connection herself helps stabilise the idea as a pattern in her mind and not just as a remark.

Batteries run flat

Grant worked as a car mechanic and found that replacing the negative metaphor he had been using with the 'flat battery' one was far more positive for him, because, as we all know, flat batteries can be recharged.

> **Grant:** It all started when I took on extra work. I started worrying about not being there enough for my wife and my daughter, who has cerebral palsy. I am worried about everything *going down the pan* and I've stopped sleeping because I know my wife is finding it hard to cope...I just have to work these extra hours at the moment—but at this rate I'm going to be signed off work and I won't get full sick pay, which makes me even more worried...

We can see from this that Grant feels he is in a typical double-bind situation—'damned if you do, damned if you don't'—with no way out. And in a state of high emotion, it is even harder to see more than two possible alternatives. If he worked, he was neglecting his home life, but if he stayed at home, he wasn't earning enough.

Therapist: You are scared of 'going down the pan', Grant, but of course people don't *really* 'go down the pan', do they? You feel depressed and exhausted?

Grant: Yes.

Therapist: Well, we won't have you going down any pan! Perhaps it's more like a battery run flat.] What happens when a car gets a flat battery from overuse? Is that the end of the car?

Grant: No. Either we recharge the battery, or we install a new one.

Therapist: And you could certainly do with a re-charged battery, right? And one of the ways we can do that is to stop worry from leaking away energy and get you properly rested and relaxed.

After a few more sessions, Grant went on to recover and never needed to fear 'going down the pan', because now all he needed to do was to 'recharge his battery'. This was a term that he could easily relate to because of his personal and professional connection to it, and he began to use it himself during the therapy. With the therapist's help, Grant and his wife organised some extra help so his wife could have some respite from looking after their daughter and so Grant could do some overtime until their debts were cleared. In this way they escaped their 'no escape' double-bind situation.

The youth of old age

Regret, or the fear of loss, is sometimes at the heart of depression. People may negatively ruminate about what they feel they have lost, or will lose. They might regret the loss of their youth, or past relationships, or mull over the future relationships they will now never have. Many of us fear getting old and losing our looks, the love of others, money, or possessions. ᖴ ○ ᗰ ○

Jacob was feeling down when he came for help. He had just turned fifty and couldn't shake the idea that it was 'all over for him'.

> **Jacob:** I just feel like I'm getting old, and I'm over the hill! I know nowadays fifty isn't old, but I can't help feeling that life has passed me by…

> **Therapist:** Yes, fifty can feel like quite a mile-stone! It reminds me of the man who said that 'forty is the old age of youth, and fifty is the youth of old age'!

Now this was just a comment, uttered as if the therapist were only thinking out loud, saying something Jacob could easily shrug off, but it contained a welcome idea, a new way of looking at his situation—i.e., that he had just entered a different phase of youthfulness—that Jacob needed.

Addiction

ﾉﾞﾞ

Addiction is a strong greed. This might sound contentious or judgmental, but it's really just descriptive. And one sure way of increasing a greed for something is to deny the person whatever it is that they are greedy for (addicted to), whether it's food, cigarettes, or alcohol. Deprivation tends to increase desire. This doesn't mean that we *can't* overcome our desire for something directly through self-deprivation, but it can be very useful in therapy to look at what it is *exactly* that someone is actually being 'deprived of'.

Deprivation

Emily was overweight. She knew what she was *supposed* to eat and how much (a lot less than she *was* eating), but she still felt that she 'deserved her treats'. She didn't snack on cakes and chocolate because she felt hungry, but because she associated these times with reward—after all, she had a demanding job and a child to care for, which could be very stressful as a single parent.

I spoke to her at length about her situation, and she admitted she was in a bind. Although she wanted to be slimmer, to wear clothes she liked, to feel sexy, and to be comfortable, she *also* felt that she would be deprived if she denied herself these 'comforts'. Clearly, she could do with a new, more useful (and more realistic) perspective on her overeating:

> **Me:** You know, you're right—why *should* you be deprived? You have a hard enough life as it is!

> **Emily:** Yes, absolutely! That's the problem. I really have very few treats…

Me: Yes, as I say, why should you be deprived… Why should you be deprived of a nice shape, of your health, of good blood pressure…You told me you used to be confident in your looks, but now, because of your weight, *you are being deprived of that confidence*. You really *don't* deserve all this deprivation.

Expanding the idea of deprivation (which Emily herself kept coming back to) allowed us to reframe her perception of the treats she was allowing herself. After this session, Emily no longer clung to her limited idea of deprivation, or to seeing her excess intake as treats.

Many people feel the same way as Emily. They don't like to feel they are being deprived of their favourite 'naughty' foods, their cigarettes, or their favourite drink, etc. But by looking at what else they are *really* being deprived of, we can widen their perspective. We can look at cigarettes, for example, as depriving people of oxygen, a pleasant odour, youth, sexual energy, and even life. Similarly, too much of the wrong food can deprive the body of comfort, movement, health, a sense of control, and feeling sexy and attractive. When someone takes time out from eating, we can reframe it as his or her digestive system having time off, or not having to do unpaid overtime, or just having space and time for itself to let things settle.

When drink is not a drink

Language is obviously important in shaping the way we perceive the world, but it also shapes how we think about our habits and problems. We can reflect with clients on how ironic it is that alcohol is called 'drink'. Drinks are something we need to survive, but alcohol is not. In fact, it can even prevent us from surviving. So to a client whose increasing reliance on alcohol was compounding his other problems, I said, "It's a very curious thing how words can get hijacked to mean different things—even their very opposite! Alcohol *steals moisture* and hydration; it *takes fluid* from the brain and bones, and *dries out* the skin and liver— yet it has become known as 'drink'! People even talk about 'having a real drink'! A sneak thief will often disguise himself as a friend."

Overflowing oestrogen lake

Sheila, a woman of forty-five, came into therapy complaining that she couldn't stop herself from drinking a bottle of wine every night when she returned from her busy and demanding job, although if she made it through to 9:00 p.m. without drinking, she would lose the urge for that night and could have an entirely clear evening.

Five years before, Sheila had had cancer, which had been '100 percent oestrogen based'. She knew that alcohol could encourage the production of oestrogen but still felt unable to stop. So I suggested to her that everyone needs some 'decompression' time after work in order to get into 'home mode'. Sometimes this is done by taking a shower or exercising, or by changing clothes—and alcohol is another way. Sheila agreed with this. We chatted further about alternative ways to decompress after work. Then she said:

Sheila: I feel so weak and pathetic drinking when I've had cancer!

Me: It can feel like weakness, yes, but all habitual patterns like drinking and smoking have a way of hypnotising us into the now, making us totally present-focussed. Every time you drink more wine, you are in fact adding to the grand total of *all* the wine you've ever drunk—like pouring wine into a huge oestrogen lake.

Sheila: Yes, when I start drinking, I kid myself that the future will never come—or I don't even think about it, because it's only now that matters.

Me: Yes, and of course this is an illusion—because every time you were drinking another bottle of wine, you were pouring more wine/ oestrogen into that lake, which may be in danger of bursting its banks at any moment and causing destruction.

This neat metaphor enabled Sheila to link each individual action to a wider consequence—so it stopped being just 'one more drink'. While she was deeply relaxed, I got her to vividly visualise the 'oestrogen lake' she was filling up each night. I also carefully referred to her drinking in the past tense: "because every time you *were* drinking" and so on.

Sheila was much taken with the metaphor of the oestrogen lake. And I didn't stop there; I described the wine as smooth and charming on the outside, but undermining and potentially damaging to her. I went on to talk about two-faced, so-called friends who seem to offer comfort but are really taking and stealing. The last time I spoke to Sheila she had been free of alcohol for two years. She is now slimmer, healthier, and satisfied with her life.

Beating the evil bottle

Eric had lost a lot through drink. He had lost his marriage and his job, and he had very limited access to the children he loved. He wanted to quit drinking but felt unable to, as it was now 'all he had left'. I asked what he would be doing if he wasn't drinking, and he said he would be doing contract design work for the companies that used to use his services. He felt pretty certain he could get work again and rebuild his life, if only he could quit.

I asked what had got him drinking in the first place. Shyness, he said. Initially drinking had made him feel confident, but although he no longer felt shy, he felt that drinking had 'cast a spell on him'.

While he was relaxed in a deep trance, I talked to Eric about the fabled genie in a bottle—about how, when initially released, the genie seems to give you anything you want, but, if you are not careful, the genie can become more powerful than you and start to go its own way. It forgets who is boss. In telling him the story of the genie, I purposely referred to the genie as the 'spirit' throughout:

Once a young man found a beautiful bottle by the seashore. Intrigued, he immediately opened it. At once an amazing and fearsome-looking genie emerged, becoming instantly much bigger than the man himself.

"I am here to help you!" bellowed the spirit.

The first thing the overjoyed man did was to order the spirit to make him renowned and talked about in his own village: "I command thee to bring me to notice, to make my name the first thing on everyone's lips tomorrow morning!"

In a flash, he found himself in the town square surrounded by all manner of people. At first he enjoyed the attention and felt that now, surely, he was at last being recognised for the great man he truly was. But then he realised that some people were pointing and laughing, and others were looking on with disgust.

"This is not the type of attention I wanted!" he shouted, before realising that he was in fact naked, and that he had been braying like a mule.

He was furious with the spirit genie that had seemed so promising. "You have made a fool of me! Come out of your bottle again and grant me a real wish!"

This time he commanded the spirit give him nothing but gold.

In a flash the spirit obeyed, and now the man found himself on an island, surrounded by gold. At first he was delighted and skipped around in glee, but soon he grew lonely and noticed that the only people there were statues made of gold! He became hungry and thirsty, but the only fruit was also made of the precious metal, and even the water in a nearby jug was metallic. It was not long before he began cursing the spirit for never really delivering what it seemed to promise.

But, even though exasperated, he could not resist having one more try. He poured the spirit genie out of its bottle once more and demanded that it find his true love and ensure that he made a big impression on her.

In less than a second he was whisked off to a wonderful palace. In the courtyard, surrounded by a throng of citizens, was the most beautiful princess. The man fell instantly in love with her, but she ignored him...at first. For the spirit had worked its twisted magic again, and the man found himself lunging at the princess and, in front of the courtiers, pressing a large rubber stamp onto her face. He had impressed her all right—literally!

Disgusted and annoyed, the princess summoned her guards. As the man was about to be taken to the dungeons, he demanded the genie help him. But by now the spirit was totally out of control and had abandoned him. Down in the darkest dungeon the man found himself in conversation with a wise old inmate, who said, "Your mistake was being loyal to the spirit genie even as it turned against you. Desperate though things may seem, there is a way to escape this." And he bent over to whisper instructions in the unhappy prisoner's ear.

Following this advice, the man escaped from that prison. After some adventures he found himself back at the very spot where he had first spied the bottle containing the genie. And lo and behold, there was the genie cavorting about in the skies above the bottle, looking for more lives to make miserable.

The man looked up and asked the spirit about himself. "I am more powerful than any man, and when I have him in my power, I can do with him what I will!" declared the spirit.

"If you are truly so powerful," said the man, "I wonder if you can prove it? I find it hard to believe, for instance, that a creature so marvellously huge could really have the power to shrink itself down again and once more fit inside this bottle!" Annoyed at this challenge, the spirit immediately shrank to a wisp and slipped into the tiny glass bottle—and, of course, no sooner had he done so than the man put the lid on again and the genie was trapped. "Now I have the power over *you*," said the man. "And because I know where it leads, I will never let you out again!"

This story stuck with Eric, and when I encountered him later, he told me he had found it relatively easy to 'keep the spirit trapped in the bottle' thereafter.

A mountain of cigarettes

Addictive behaviours focus us totally on the present moment. Future consequences evaporate in the rush to satisfy the immediate desire. Addictive rituals such as smoking cigarettes become 'bubbles in time', cursed but also somehow treasured escapes from future thought or consideration. For someone to stop, they have to *feel* the weight of the future keenly as they try to smoke.

Robert was nearly forty, an office administrator. He had been a keen mountaineer in his youth but now smoked thirty to forty cigarettes a day. He knew that he shouldn't smoke, as he had lost fitness and was aging more rapidly because of the smoking, but he said it always seemed like 'just one' couldn't really hurt. He always felt he could quit tomorrow (which, of course, never comes) because, after all, 'one couldn't hurt'. Robert was hypnotised and as he focussed deep in trance, his therapist said:

> You know, Robert, after the first cigarette you smoked when you were fourteen, it is never 'just one' anymore because…they all join together. You have smoked hundreds of thousands of cigarettes

in your life; thousands upon thousands have conned their way into you. In fact, if you could see all the cigarettes you'd ever smoked together, there'd be a mountain of them! So now you never just smoke one, you smoke one *on top of all the others*. And that mountain grows and grows. It is never just one.

And as you continue to add cigarettes to that mountain, it starts to become unstable, and of course, as the pressure builds, that mountain could collapse and bury you! When you've stopped being manipulated by cigarettes into thinking 'it's just one', then you can begin to *move away from that mountain* until such time as it's in the distance, and so far over the horizon that you'll forget about it entirely.

But if you ever have one in future, you can be transported right back to that unstable mountain of all the cigarettes you'd ever smoked.

Intelligent rebellion

When we force ourselves *not* to do something, we build an inner tension. This is like forcing an elastic band in one direction. Eventually the elastic rebels against the tension and flies back the other way *because* we were trying to force it beyond its tolerance—the 'elastic band effect'. Telling a teenage girl *not* to see a boy she is infatuated with will likely increase her desire to see him; you pull her one way, and she becomes more attracted to going the other way— the elastic springs back again. Telling people they *shouldn't* smoke or drink when so much of such addictive behaviour is about rebelling against advice and orders can, paradoxi- cally, encourage them to carry on with the activity.

When treating people with addictions, we need to address this aspect of rebellion and bring it out into the open so we can deal with it and redirect it. People often begin smok- ing, for example, as an adolescent behaviour, as something forbidden with which they can assert their independence. To tell them not to do it makes it even more deliciously forbidden.

It's interesting, how so many people get conned by cigarettes into using *them* to rebel with. You know the scenario: "Oh, what the hell, I've had a crap day, what difference will one make?" Or: "Who are they to tell me not to smoke?!" And, you know, rebellion is fine as long as it's *intelligent* rebellion, and you rebel against what's *really* undermining and stealing from you. A repressive dictatorship will always seek to get its population opposing *other* systems of government, so that the people won't actually rebel against what is really repressing them. So let's make sure we have intelligent rebellion!

I don't want to be manipulated

When faced with a rebellious smoker, you can often build rapport and show an understanding of his or her feelings and position by preempting any objections and likely areas of resistance he or she might be thinking of. Raising and dealing with any possible objections like this brings you together as a team and helps to weaken the pull of those objections, clearing the ground for effective therapeutic work.

Dan was keen to stop smoking. He was pleasant, but in a truculent sort of way, and had a glint in his eye that spoke volumes. "I really do want to stop smoking—but don't you *dare* give me platitudes!" his manner seemed to say. As we chatted about his situation, he suddenly said, "I just can't stand it when people tell me I should quit! It's like a police state or something. I want to quit in my own way, not be manipulated into it!"

I answered back immediately:

> Of course you don't want to be manipulated! Who'd want to be like someone who joins a cult, and the cult really takes over his life, stealing from

him? For that to somehow get to be okay for him, the victim has to buy into certain beliefs, so that he can continue being manipulated. Though, you know, I do see this with some smokers. It's like, in order for them to be successfully taken in by smoking, they have to bolster their behaviour with certain beliefs until they see through it.

Typical cult beliefs of smoking they might hold are that smokers are more interesting, intellectual, cool, or bohemian, or that smoking relaxes them, or that it's such a fascinating activity that it relieves boredom, or is intrinsically part of who they are, you know, like their identity is built up around a toxic leaf! Or that it's so ecstatically enjoyable that it is worth throwing away their youth and life for, or that you can only take a break if you smoke, or that it's very physically addictive, or that it's a natural accompaniment to tea, coffee, alcohol, or postcoitus.

Some people even think that it's worth continuing just to spite antismokers. Or they declare that they could easily die in a car crash tomorrow anyway (though they should *really* look at the statistical probabilities of that happening!), or that their uncle Freddie lived to two hundred eighty, smoked a thousand cigs a day, and ran record marathons!

116

> Buying into all or any of these types of belief on any level certainly manipulates people, and it doesn't surprise me that you *don't* want to be manipulated, do you...

This kind of free-flowing soliloquy preempts some of the likely objections the smoker may have and leaves him few excuses to cling to! When we present beliefs as *standard*, *predictable*, and *conditioned* into lots of people, then they become less tenable to the person and therefore less likely to persist, because they have been found out.

This is not to dictate to clients what they can or should believe—that would be likely to set them up in opposition to *you* instead of the smoking, and so break rapport. Instead, you are just presenting another way of looking at the situation by talking about *other people*: "You know, *some people think...*" If those 'some people' happen to include the person in front of you, then all the better. If they haven't been wound up by a confrontational approach, they will be calmer and more able to absorb what you're saying.

The 'abusive relationship'

Most people can relate to the reality of abusive relationships, but few like to admit they themselves have ever fallen prey to a sweet-talking swindler, whether in a relationship or some other context, such as a financial deal.

Caroline was single and hadn't been in a relationship for 'a while'. But this wasn't why she went to a therapist. She had stopped smoking twice before and now wanted to do so again. The first time she had stopped for three months and the second for a whole year, but she said she had 'always gone back to them'. As she talked, she referred to cigarettes as 'a friend' and a supportive crutch, always there to rely on. Half an hour into the session, her therapist said:

> You know, people sometimes get into an abusive relationship. It often seems OK at first, but pretty soon it starts becoming clear that the abusive partner is undermining them, taking money from them, and maltreating them. You've probably seen this happen to someone you know. Despite this, he or she may still have a bit of starry-eyed naivety

around his or her partner—perhaps because of the way things used to be. Everyone else can see clearly that they should give that partner the boot.

Eventually, they make the break, and usually feel pretty pleased they did. But it often happens, maybe a few months later, when they are maybe feeling a little bored, or tired, or lonely, and lo and behold, that their ex-partner phones them up! And they are so glad to hear that voice again because *at that moment* they just remember the good times.

So if their ex-partner then says, "Hey, why don't we just have one date, just a drink—nothing more?", they think, "Why not? It won't mean anything!" And then, before you know it, they're back together and the same old abusive pattern has started up again.

Well, smoking will try and do the same, because it sees *you* as a good bet. Because not everyone is prepared to give it a home while it destroys them and pay good money for the privilege! So, you need to be ready for it when it tries to whisper in your ear next time…and you can be prepared…because it will try to get you back again.

This metaphor picked up on Caroline's own description of smoking in terms of a 'relationship' and reframed smoking as an abusive relationship—with her as the victim. It also planted the idea that this time she would be ready and 'see through the lies' when it tried to get her back again.

The stupid parasite that destroys its own home

Smokers—or victims of nicotine—don't like to be told they are 'cruising for a bruising' and are likely to be 'sacrificed' for their smoking beliefs, so another useful metaphor for reframing the harm that smoking does is to present tobacco as a parasite. Despite all the evidence before them, people are not generally *frightened* into quitting smoking (just think how many committed smokers you see standing outside hospital pulmonary wards, puffing in the cold), because of the elastic band effect referred to earlier. But you can sometimes bypass such resistance by shocking them into seeing and absorbing the truth about their situation in a totally new way, with a startlingly different yet pertinent metaphor that is such a surprise it 'wakes them up'. For example: "And you know, continuing to feed that spoilt nicotine parasite is bad for you, of course, but also bad for it! Bad for you for obvious reasons, but bad for the nicotine because it is systematically making itself homeless by destroying its own home."

If smoking is a parasite that nests within people demanding to be fed, then (and this is the real shock) it makes sense that by killing its hosts it has done itself a *huge* disservice by making itself homeless. Crazy, but memorable!

You don't have to be antismoking

Many people don't like the idea that in giving up smoking they may become an antismoker—a breed they often regard as boorish and extreme. So I'll often let people know that I'm not antismoking myself; it's just that I'm against people being taken in or predictably manipulated by something that steals so much from them while they pay cash for the privilege! The following interchange is a typical example where I threw in similar reframes.

Jim: [*still smoking, and defiant*] I suppose you *hate* smokers!

Me: Not at all! Of course people should smoke, if what they get from it is worth the cost and consequences. If it's *genuinely* the most rewarding and pleasurable aspect of someone's existence, I am all for people smoking. But the problem is that some people *don't* find it pleasurable enough to make it worthwhile, and *that* is what I am against. I can't stand the fanatical antismoking brigade myself. You know, if a person *hates* someone, or something, this indicates he or she is still very involved with what he or she hates; hate is a type of intimacy and connection. When you've really seen through smoking [*a useful way to reframe stopping smoking*] then you can genuinely be indifferent and unconcerned about it…and that's true liberation and the proper end to an abusive relationship.

Jim: Oh! Well…that's good!

By reframing being *anti*smoking as still being too *attached* to smoking, I had allowed Jim to relax about becoming a nonsmoker, and to see it as a new identity he could comfortably adopt.

Withdrawal as healing time

Ian was also concerned about withdrawal from nicotine. Although we know that the vast majority of people quit smoking without severe withdrawal symptoms, this is still a major fear for many people who would like to give up. So, rather than talk to Ian about withdrawal, with its implications of suffering and unpleasant denial, I talked about his body's 'healing time' after quitting. With good justification, we can reframe the period after stopping as a time when the body is 'healing up'. Healing is a concept we are all familiar with. It implies positive action for the body and also, importantly, that there will be a time when the healing process is finished and everything is fully healed and healthy again.

So while Ian was deeply relaxed, I said, "And your body has already begun to heal…and you can really notice the signs of that healing over the next few days…before being free of them becomes a habit itself."

'Self-harm'

Reframes can make people aware of how addictions trick them, and they can sometimes shock people into realising the harm they are doing to themselves. This can sometimes provide motivation enough for them to change their behaviour, especially if you give them an alternative image to conjure up that will override their current expectation of the pleasure to be derived from their particular addictive behaviour.

Most people wouldn't consider themselves self-harmers, even if they smoke. But reframing smoking as self-harm can prove very powerful. Seeing familiar patterns in unfamiliar ways helps give us the necessary detachment to see what is really going on: it's shocking to hear yourself likened to someone you wouldn't ever consider yourself to be like.

"I'm not like that!"

James was one such young man; he absolutely loved sport but was damaging his own health and performance by continuing to smoke a packet of cigarettes a day. He sat across from me in my therapy room and we chatted for a while before even broaching the subject of cigarettes. While giving me background to his life, James told me, rather contemptuously, about a 'crazy ex-girlfriend' who had been admitted to a psychiatric unit after cutting her own arms and legs. I deliberately showed little sympathy for her in my response:

> **Me:** That's interesting! You know, I used to work in a psychiatric hospital. Some of the cutters we had there would sit down with a cup of tea in front of their favourite TV show and start cutting. Some would cut five, ten, or more times a day. Of course, we tried to prevent it, but these cutters could be crafty and would sometimes sneak sharp objects in. Before working there, I assumed self-harmers hacking away at their skins would be very wound up when they got their fix. So it kind of shocked

me to see how *casual* the self-harm could be. How long have *you* been self-harming?

James: I don't self-harm!

Me: I mean the smoking. It's amazing how many people self-harm with cigarettes rather than blades…How long have *you* been self-harming?

James was shocked but subdued after that. For the rest of the session I referred to self-harm instead of smoking. When I saw him again, James told me he hadn't had a single cigarette since before our last session. As he got up to go this time, he told me he just couldn't smoke anymore, because it was self-harm: "I'm just not like that!"

Healthy Laziness

Many people feel that stopping smoking is hard work. So to help clients who are put off by the thought of the effort required, we can suggest the opposite—that *not* doing something is actually the easy option and a form of inertia, whereas smoking requires planning, effort, and activity. "I am going to stop smoking" is actually equivalent, therefore, to "I am going to not exercise" or "I am going to not make dinner anymore".

Smoking bodies

It's often helpful to explore the idea of smoking itself in greater depth. For instance, the body itself never 'smokes' unless it is actually set on fire! Likewise, smoking is not a natural bodily process, like digestion or mineral absorption; all the body does when nicotine is consumed is try to reject the toxins as quickly as possible!

Disgusting tenants

Smoking is not a good deal: you pay for something to damage you! It wouldn't be so bad if you got money for 'housing' the tobacco parasite. This reframe can help smokers see their habit in a new light: "And imagine having tenants on your property that not only refuse to pay you, but are filthy and messy and manipulate *you* into paying *them* on a weekly basis! Not only that, but they *steal* from you [*money, youth, energy, smell and taste, mobility, etc*]. So today let's look at really kicking those squatters out and clearing up the house that *you* live in and pay for!"

Heroin-scoring monkeys

Apart from the health risks associated with heroin injection itself, the very state of being heavily addicted can destroy someone's life, as funding and sourcing such a habit leaves little time for loved ones, a career, or a social life beyond the circle of other users. Heroin demands more and more in the way of money, time, health, and self-respect.

I went to see Debbie at home to help her quit the 'love of her life', as she described it. She was bone thin and desperately worried because the social services were considering taking her neglected four-year-old into care. Month-old unwashed dishes were stacked up in the kitchen, the air was musty, the curtains were drawn, and there was a general feeling of age and decay all around, even though Debbie was only thirty-five.

She told me she had been working and had managed to save up enough for a deposit on a house, but had been signed off sick these past six months to get herself straight and off the heroin. She told me that she loved her son but found release in scoring her fix. She realised she was now starting to spend precious food and housekeeping money on her habit, and unless she could cut down and eventually quit, she would lose her son. She was being assisted in her withdrawal by a drugs worker, but was secretly scoring without this person's knowledge.

I asked Debbie if she loved heroin more than her son. She looked shocked and didn't reply. I asked her to close her eyes and imagine her son. A slight smile slowly spread across her wan face and grew into a beam as I described his own smile and love of her. I then asked her to picture heroin as if it were a person or being—what would it look like? I commented on how it had charmed and conned her and was leading her to destruction. She started to frown faintly and later reported that a dirty, smelly, Grim Reaper type image had come to mind—and that it had looked just like her ex-husband!

I suggested that a river trip on a canoe could be pleasurable for a while, but that there might well be a cascading waterfall around the bend. I then told her this story:

Once there was a monkey. This monkey was in some ways good and in some ways greedy. His greed meant that he was always looking for shortcuts to feeling good. Other monkeys would search diligently for their food, but he would attempt to steal theirs without putting in any work of his own.

One day as he was out and about he came across a strange thing. A juicy pineapple lay before him inside a glass jar. He immediately put his paw into the jar and grabbed the fruit. However, with his fist clenched tight around it, he couldn't remove the pineapple and free his arm from the jar. He pulled and struggled, looking back over his shoulder at the safety of the trees. But the pineapple would not come out of the jar. And he was far too greedy to let go. And it was not long before the hunter came out of hiding, and the monkey's fate was sealed.

I suggested to Debbie that she relax further, and when she was deeply relaxed, I helped her to rehearse in her imagination refusing the dealer's offers of more heroin, and then playing with her son and spending the money saved on food and building their future. Later, as she drifted out of trance, she smiled at me, looking like the young, intelligent woman she was, and said, "No one has ever had the guts to call me greedy before!"

Buying your own sweets

As we've seen, trying *not* to do something is all well and good but still creates tension through the rubber band effect. If you leave the band entirely alone, no tension is created. This analogy is relevant to the addict in withdrawal when he or she is trying not to indulge addiction—far better for something to become irrelevant than to build up pressure by trying *not* to do it. Ironically, one client I knew had become addicted to rubber bands themselves!

Sadie was in her late forties. She lived alone in a nice flat and had a good job, but she admitted to me shamefacedly that she had a quite disgusting habit, which she just couldn't seem to break. When she was sure no one was looking, she would scan the street for discarded cigarettes that still had 'some smoke in them'. She would pick them up and surreptitiously smoke them and feel initially satisfied but then quite appalled at herself.

She didn't usually smoke and certainly had enough money to buy her own cigarettes if she chose. What was worse in her eyes (and possibly even more unhygienic) was that if she happened to find a discarded rubber band anywhere (in the street, at her office, etc) she would find some opportunity to pop it in her mouth and chew it for hours. She desperately wanted to stop both these patterns.

Therapist: So, Sadie, why do you do this, do you suppose?

Sadie: I think I know why. My mother died when I was very young. My father remarried and I had the proverbial 'wicked stepmother'. She would make a point of never giving me a gift on my birthday or Christmas, and I was never allowed sweets like other children. I was ashamed and embarrassed about never having sweets to bring to school and would watch to see if any were ever left or even spilt onto the ground. If they were, I would wait until no one was looking and then sweep them up and enjoy this naughty pleasure. My stepmother would also continually chastise me for chewing on elastic bands—it really irritated her.

[*NB: Sadie had a good idea why she had developed the problem behaviour, but this insight hadn't been enough to stop her from engaging in it. Some therapists assume that once we know why we have a problem, the problem naturally dissolves. This is rarely the case.*]

Therapist: OK, Sadie. And when you think about that little girl, what comes to mind?

Sadie: A feeling, really, just the feeling that I want my share, that it's not fair, and why do I always have to scrabble around in the dirt and pick up other people's leftovers?

Therapist: Now here is what I want you to do. I want you to go and buy some rubber bands and scatter them on the floor at home. Every day, until we next see each other, you can pick one from the floor and chew it, but as you chew, you are to say out loud, "I can get my own sweets, I can get my own sweets."

The therapist had nurtured sufficient trust and rapport with Sadie for her to agree to this rather strange course of action. The following week she reported that after only three days she no longer felt like picking the elastic bands up from the floor and chewing them, and had seen several discarded cigarettes lying in the street and not even been tempted to smoke them. She wept in the session while saying, smiling, that she always cried a little whenever she said good-bye to something forever. The therapist suggested that what serves us well for one part of our life can cease to be useful when we have grown up. For this woman, the repeated thought, "I can buy my own sweets", helped break the troublesome pattern of behaviour and allowed her to move on in her life, eventually getting into a happy relationship, travelling to exotic lands, and truly looking after the real needs of her body.

One more cup of coffee for the road

Caffeine is the most widely used drug in the world. People get hooked on their daily (or even hourly) hit and use it to focus, socialise, and keep working. As with most things, moderate use of caffeine doesn't seem to have too much downside. But too much caffeine (three cups of strong coffee or more) can cause insomnia, irritability, migraine, loss of concentration, anxiety, osteoporosis, diabetes, ulcers, PMS, stroke, and heart disease, and may even be linked to certain types of cancer. Heavy coffee users say they often feel exhausted, but edgy at the same time. Overstimulation can lead to tiredness, but the excess caffeine in the bloodstream can prevent rest.

Jerry came to me because he felt stressed out. I questioned him in detail about his lifestyle. He was currently working up to sixteen hours a day to meet a looming deadline. His diet wasn't too bad, but he told me he was drinking up to twenty cups of filter coffee a day—sometimes more. He had been to see his doctor, complaining of a racing heart, but had been told to just try and take it easy. So we looked at changing key elements of his working day. I taught him how to relax very deeply very quickly, so that he could do a ten-minute relaxation every afternoon after the lunch he was to make sure to take each day. He had a love of cars, which I knew about from having already spoken at some length on the telephone. (I had done my homework!) So next I addressed the coffee issue.

Me: You know, Jerry, some people would say, and they would be right, that twenty cups of coffee a day is way too much!

Jerry: I know what you mean, but I don't think it's actually been making that much difference to me.

Me: Are you a human being?

Jerry: [*laughing*] In some ways!

Me: Well, do you have a central nervous system?

Jerry: Most definitely. That's why I've been getting so nervous.

Me: Let me put it another way. You love your car, right? Cars are a passion of yours, and it's great if they run efficiently, and, of course, cost effectively, right? You want to be fuel-injected, not carburetted, do you not?

[Jerry looked at me with a glint in his eyes—he knew what I was getting at.]

Your knowledge is far greater than mine, but as I understand it, the old carburetted systems only consider engine vacuum and throttle position, with an indirect method for determining when the engine is first being started. This is, of course, far less energy efficient, as the engine can take up more fuel than it really needs. Fuel injection actually monitors what's going on in the engine, right? Delivering the proper amount of fuel to provide maximum power for the minimum amount of fuel. Fuel injection is far more efficient and produces far fewer unwanted emissions...if you know what I mean. How long are you going to inject fuel you don't need with all the wear and tear that is going to cause?

I actually had rather little idea of what I was talking about, but Jerry did. I had linked his interest in the smooth running of his cars to his vast overconsumption of strong coffee. This was an idea he couldn't forget because it was expressed in *his* terms, using *his* frames of reference. I felt that it deepened our rapport, as I had obviously taken the trouble to think about car fuel systems while conceding that he was the expert. Henceforth he would talk about his 'fuel efficiency' when referring to coffee consumption. He gradually cut down to the 'efficient level'.

Scoring points

Barbara brought her twenty-two-year-old son, Gary, in for help. She told me despairingly that her son lived at home with her, no longer worked, and spent all his time on 'bloody computer games'. Gary himself told me he was hooked and didn't even enjoy playing the games anymore, but that he still couldn't stop thinking about his high scores. I discussed with him the things his life was lacking at the moment (a job, a circle of friends or colleagues, direction, real challenge, etc), and we agreed that the obsessive gaming was both a possible consequence of his life not being full enough, and also something that was in turn *preventing* these needs from being fulfilled.

Me: So, Gary, how many points would a girlfriend be?

Gary: What?!

Me: Well, if we were to assign scores to the things your life is lacking—the 'game of life', if you like— how many points would a girlfriend be?

Gary: Well, that would be the highest score, then!

I then got him to assign a score value to all the things currently lacking in his life (analogous to the scoring system of the game he was currently obsessing over). I suggested that a day of *not* playing would surely be worth a lot, as it was a step towards 'getting a life', as he had called it. He took this idea further and assigned a point score to not playing for a whole day, and then a whole week, and then a month. I asked him to e-mail me each day with his 'score', which he did diligently. Three months later he had a job, had enrolled on a part-time course, and was 'getting close to a certain girl'. I resisted suggesting to him that he might 'score'.

The true flavour

Human beings can get used to anything. If we repeat something often enough, it can start to feel familiar and we can train ourselves to feel that we like it, or convince ourselves that it is necessary, even essential. Adam came in for help as a 'committed smoker'.

Adam: I just love smoking. I want to stop, but the trouble is I just love the taste, and I don't think I've got the willpower to give up!

Me: And that *is* curious, because you certainly need willpower…to smoke…because when you first start it's disgusting, and to keep going you have to get over the sensation that you are wrapping your lips around a car exhaust pipe! You needed willpower to keep going to overcome your body's first true and honest response to that poison. So willpower is not the problem. And I wonder if you can recall now, or at least if your body can recall, a time when you puffed on that poison for the very first time, and you had to be determined to overcome that initial revulsion.

It can be useful to vividly reevoke a memory of the first contact with the now-addictive behaviour *before it became addictive*. In this way part of the pattern can begin to become deconstructed, dismantled, and the addictive pattern can be reframed as something that a person at one time (especially in the case of smoking) had to *force* himself to do.

When the same is different

When dealing with addictive behaviour, it's important to consider how stuck a person can become in the trance-like, almost mechanical act of continuing the pattern past the point of satisfaction or enjoyment. This is the 'chocolate box syndrome': some people can enjoy one or two chocolates and leave the rest for another time, but there are many who feel it would be impossible to do this, expressing the sentiment that if it is there, they *have* to have it!

Even when we overindulge occasionally, we can do most things safely in moderation. It's only when we start doing them compulsively that binge mentality has taken hold. The very first chocolate may seem slightly different from the second or third, but if we're bingeing, it can be completely different from the last, which by then may have lost all its flavour and texture to us as we force it down. We can savour the first because it *is* the first and we are acting out of choice, but the last is a completely different animal.

In such cases, I might ask someone to close his or her eyes and imagine tasting the very first chocolate, and then to imagine forcing down the very last one while really *noticing* the difference. We can then ask that person when the enjoyment of eating chocolates would start to diminish as it is taken over by compulsion. Would it be after the second, or the third, or the fourth? By doing this we are negotiating a point at which he or she can be trained to stop. And it will be more enjoyable this way. This is not the same as telling someone that they must *never* eat chocolate again, and so helps avoid the aforementioned elastic band effect that self-denial can produce.

A near miss

Graham went to a therapist because, with the help of his doctor, he had stopped drinking completely but was having problems. He had been a very heavy drinker, and the drinking had started to make him very ill. But now he was tempted to 'go back to the booze' because he couldn't stand the 'side effects' of not drinking. He particularly hated the DTs (delirium tremens, or shaking) that he was experiencing. At the same time, he was very aware that, if he did drink again, before long it would kill him.

> **Graham:** Listen, I simply can't stand this shaking. Look at me! It's not right, and sometimes, I can tell you, I think it would be easier to go back to the drinking!

> **Therapist:** What did your doctor say to you about what drinking would do to your body if you continued?

> **Graham:** She said that I could die within six months.

> **Therapist:** And you want to live?

Graham: Yes, of course! I have a wife who loves me and young children whom I want to be there for as they grow up.

Therapist: And you find the healing process unpleasant...but it *is* a healing process [*withdrawal is here reframed as healing*]. Your body must be so relieved that you are giving it a chance to live! And when we have had a near miss, we do shake for a while...

Graham actually laughed out loud at this idea—but as he said later, he just couldn't get the thought out of his head that his body was just 'shaking with relief' at its close escape.

A cutting remark

People who self-harm do so for a variety of reasons. Many start because it gives them a momentary sense of relief, through turning their attention from feelings of desperation, depression, or anxiety. So self-harming is an attempted solution, but it can also have an addictive element. And like any addictive behaviour, there is often a buildup of tension before the self-harming binge, followed by initial feelings of relief that are often swiftly replaced with feelings of regret and sometimes self-disgust afterwards.

After years of cutting herself, Karen went for help when she had finally reached the point where she couldn't bear to have yet another skin graft to cover the scars—especially as she was now 'running out of skin' to have grafted. Yet still she kept cutting. Part of her wanted to quit, but another part felt that, as it was *her* skin, why *shouldn't* she have the say over whether she cut it or not?

> **Karen:** I know I should quit, and I know everyone else has got my best interests at heart and all that, but I *do* feel that they should mind their own business. After all, it is *my* skin.

Therapist: Absolutely. I was wondering, Karen, do you have any pets? Any 'companion animals'?

Karen: Yes. I have two beautiful cats.

Therapist: Oh, I love cats. And I have one of my own. If I wanted to skin that cat alive, what would you think of me?

Karen: That would be terrible! You could *never* do that!

Therapist: No, I certainly could never do anything like that. But they are *my* cats. They belong to me…And your skin belongs to you. It is under your care. It relies on you to look after it, to protect it. Other 'interfering' people may try to prevent cruelty to cats and well they might…Because when I own something, I am also responsible for it.

This may sound confrontational, even shocking, but by this point the therapist had built a very good level of rapport with Karen. The therapist reframed her skin as something she owned and needed to protect and be responsible for. This idea went a long way towards helping her achieve a more objective perspective and become more detached and 'outside' of her self-harming behaviour.

That elastic band again

The elastic band analogy can be particularly useful for people who have been addicted and are attempting to force themselves through willpower to stay clean. The more you pull in one direction, the more the elastic wants to ping back in the other. Pressure builds, which is why someone may force herself not to smoke for weeks, then suddenly find that the craving builds and she 'pings back'—relapses—and starts smoking again.

Sue was much taken with this metaphor. She felt it was an accurate description of her own bulimic bingeing pattern. But the analogy, while descriptive and easy for people to relate to, isn't as positive in and of itself as we'd like.

> **Sue:** Yes, that's exactly how it is! At first I'm able to stop myself from bingeing easily, but as I force myself not to do it for days and days, the pressure builds up more and more to do it. It's just like that elastic band getting tighter and wanting to release back. So how on earth will I ever be free of it?

> **Me:** Well, people do become free of it. Of course, it's much better to feel you have just grown beyond

a pattern of behaviour and that it no longer sits with who you are. But even people who force themselves not to do something can reach the point where the elastic either snaps and you are free of the pattern suddenly, or it just loses its elasticity and will never spring back anymore.

This was useful for Sue. She had liked and recognised the elastic band analogy as reflecting her own experience of compulsion. By then extending the analogy in an undeniable way (elastic bands *do* snap or lose their elasticity), she could accept that change was possible, and that *not* doing something for long enough could eventually make it easy not to do it, rather than it being a continuous, self-enforced strain.

Case study – Carol and her 'pleasure'

❧

This full case history is included as a detailed example of a complete therapy session incorporating reframing and the elaboration of related metaphors.

Carol was a smoker. She really liked smoking and didn't see why she should stop; her hacking cough was 'just a cough', after all, and apparently she'd 'always' got breathless climbing the stairs. In fact, Carol was only in front of me now because her fiancé really wanted her to quit.

"I have to have some pleasure in life, don't I?" she said, with a conspiratorial and yet rather defiant smile.

I smiled back and said, "Absolutely! You have to have some pleasure [matching her sentiment], and the pleasure surely must be *exquisite*!" She looked startled. My initial agreement, when she had expected contradiction, had caught her off guard. "You must be shrieking with pleasure from the rooftops; it must be the greatest meaning in your life, every cigarette an intense, orgasmic, fulfilling snippet of paradise! Nothing less. Because, if it isn't *that* pleasurable, some would argue you are getting the raw end of a bad deal!"

The deal

Carol looked at me, nonplussed. She was unsure of whether I had agreed with her that she should smoke—and unsure of whether she liked me.

"What deal?" she asked.

"Well," I continued, "if smoking is just 'quite nice' or 'quite relaxing', then that's not really good enough. The 'deal', as I see it, is this:

"On your part, *you* give the cigarettes your youth, your breath, your serotonin—which it destroys, so making you more prone to depression and physical pain. You give it your healthy cells, your arteries, the years from the end of your life, your gums, which it rots, and your eyesight, which it dims. You give it your looks, your money, the health of your ovaries, your skin's elasticity, your bone density, and your blood flow—which it blocks. It gets all that, and I would say that's a fair deal *if*, and *only if*, the pleasure you get from it is *unbelievably* exquisite and intense. If it's just 'OK' or even 'really good', then that's still a very poor deal for you."

155

Carol stared at me in amazement as I asked her, "If ten is the score for the most exquisite, intense pleasure you can possibly imagine, and one is the score for just plain normal, how many ten-scoring cigarettes would you say you have in any one day?"

"None are ten. I suppose the one in the evening after dinner might get a four..."

"OK. But I hope there aren't any cigarettes that slip through the net—the ones you smoke while driving, or standing out in the rain, say, without even really noticing them worming their way in—because, if you ever smoke like that, then you are giving away all that and getting even less back for your exchange! If *all* the cigarettes in your day make a four, then maybe that's good enough—maybe you should see the deal through to the end!"

Carol spoke again: "But of course not! I already said some were less than a four!"

Those prepared to lay down their lives for the greater 'good'

This conversation was so unexpected, confusing, and different that Carol's attention had become fully focussed. The slight frown and look of puzzlement on her face indicated that her fixed mind-set was perhaps already starting to loosen.

"But there is another way of looking at it," I continued. "It's not my job to tell you not to smoke—after all, you are a grown woman, not the fourteen-year-old this habit really belongs to. Anyone who is prepared to make the ultimate sacrifice, prepared to lay down her life for a cause, is worthy of respect, whether that person is among the Japanese kamikaze pilots who threw their lives away for the 'greater cause' by crashing their planes into enemy war ships, or terrorists willing to die for their beliefs in the name of religion. Happily for the tobacco companies, there are *still* smokers who are prepared to die for the greater cause of tobacco profits. If people weren't prepared to lay down their lives for the tobacco giants, how could these industries continue to make a profit? But fortunately for them,

there are people like you, who are happy to make the ultimate sacrifice for their cause—the pursuit of money."

I uttered all this in a laid-back, friendly, almost jokey way
that jarred with the content of what I was saying and thus
further focussed her attention. These 'crazy ideas' are only
crazy on one level: the tobacco industry *does* need people
willing to endanger themselves and potentially die for
them in order for the business to prosper. Carol knew that
I wasn't lying about that.

Although the way I presented this idea was unusual, Carol
needed something new, as she'd heard all the 'don't smoke'
rhetoric before. She had come in expecting more 'don't
smoke, it's bad for you' platitudes, but instead she was getting a weird kind of encouragement. She didn't know what
to think. If she rebelled against me now, it would imply
that she would need to carry on being prepared to sacrifice herself for other people's financial benefit. By using
this surprising reframe and the associated analogies, I was
connecting with her *emotional* mind, not the logical part,
which could so easily argue itself out of a box (or possibly
into one).

Dictatorships

By startling her like this, I had first focussed her attention, and by continuing to talk to her in this confusing way, I had soon led her into a trance, which I then deepened with suggestions for relaxation and dissociation. Then I continued to introduce new metaphors.

"A dictatorship is a system that seeks to control the population it rules. A small part of the overall collective at the top controls the working conditions, living conditions, and eventual fate of all the other 'parts' of that system. Now, a long time ago, that smoking dictator began demanding, manipulating, and controlling all those different parts of the overall system. You can think of your body as a population. That heart—which has always been loyal to you— never asked to be squeezed and pushed around and bullied by the nicotine; it had no choice! And if it had freedom of speech under this dictatorship, which is cruelly preventing it from beating to its maximum potential, I wonder what it would finally say to you, if it had a voice, some representation at last."

I sat back and watched as Carol—defender of cigarettes, sceptic of do-gooder therapists and 'health freaks'—sat and 'listened' to her own heart. (After all, she was more likely to listen to herself than to me!) And then I continued:

"And what would your lungs—who have loyally been trying to fulfil the allotted number of lifetime breaths for you, who just want to do their job without interference and sabotage—what would *they* say if they finally had a voice concerning the conditions they have been forced to live under by that nicotine dictator? Listen to your lungs now, because maybe they are ready to rebel against this maltreatment, and maybe they need someone to finally liberate them."

Again she sat as if she were listening to her lungs talk to her about the smoking.

I then focussed on her hands. "Now those hands resting there on your lap. They depend on the heart and lungs for their continued existence, because they won't always be here, but they want to be here for as long as possible. It's not in their interests to pick up those cigarettes to betray the heart and lungs and cells of your body. Regardless of what you think *you* want, those hands *don't* want to betray the body by colluding with that lying, cheating, thieving, smoking dictator, that betrayer nicotine, who pretends to be such a friend."

160

Reluctant hands and the final straw

"Because you're going to find those hands become numb with reluctance when it comes to taking a hand against the heart and lungs…like the straw that breaks the camel's back…because you never know which one it's going to be…which one, on top of all the others, is going to do the final irreversible damage…because it could be any one of them that makes everything too late for your loyal heart and lungs."

The condemned prisoner

"And like a prisoner who really wants to live, but is forced to dig his own grave by the very captors he thought he was in love with, whom he wouldn't hear a word against… dragging and numb and heavy with reluctance at that enforced task, those hands are going to be numb with reluctance, because you never know which one it's going to be…Whenever even the thought of colluding with that tobacco industry and betraying those loyal parts of your body occurs…"

While she was still deeply relaxed in hypnosis, I encouraged Carol to picture herself at times and in situations when typically before she would have smoked. However, I didn't refer to her as smoking in those situations, but as being 'pushed around' or 'manipulated'. This language ensured that she saw the cigarettes as something apart from her own identity, and therefore something towards which she could usefully direct her inclination to rebel.

At the end of the session Carol beamed at me, said she felt 'strange, but good', and left.

Two years later, she phoned to book an appointment for a friend. "By the way, I haven't smoked since our session!" she said. "My hands won't let me. Oh, and my friend really doesn't want to quit, so you'll have no trouble with her!"

Good things to remem-
ber when doing therapy

- Maintain good rapport with your clients.

- Normalise their situations.

- Emphasise that their situations are temporary (if realistic).

- Show that things can be different.

- Pay attention to the language and images they use and utilise them yourself.

- Metaphorical reframes are often more power-ful than direct reframes, as they bypass poten-tial left-brain, analytical resistance. Because they are not consciously connected to any-thing the client has just said, they don't seem like contradiction, and they can help maintain rapport. They can be used at any time after the client has expressed limiting ideas.

- Scatter approach: use as many stories, metaphors, reframes, etc, as possible, as you can never know exactly which will 'take'.

- Relax and let your own creativity flourish!

More resources

If you'd like more ideas for therapy, please come over to my blog at http://www.unk.com/blog and subscribe to my weekly therapy techniques newsletter, *Clear Thinking*.

I also have an audio training product on reframing, which you can read more about here: http://www.hypnosisdownloads.com/cdtape/reframing

For training in the rewind technique, rapid depression treatment, smoking cessation, and more, see our training courses here: http://www.unk.com/u/

[1] Shah, I. (1991) *World Tales*, Octagon Press Ltd.

[2] To remove phobias or detraumatise someone, I use a very effective technique called the 'rewind'. The rewind technique involves

reviewing the problematic event/s while in a state of deep relaxation and dissociation, so that the traumatic memories can be reprocessed in the brain as normal past memories, rather than remaining tagged by the amygdala as 'current realities' and so constantly triggering the fight-or-flight response. It is beyond the remit of this book to give a full account of the rewind technique—which is effective even when the therapist doesn't know all the details of the trauma—but it is an essential part of the skills base of a modern therapist, and I thoroughly recommend you train in its use. See: www.unk.com/rewind

[3] Griffin, J. and Tyrrell, I. (2000) *The APET Model: Patterns in the brain*, HG Publishing.

[4] Griffin, J. and Tyrrell, I. (2003) *Human Givens: A new approach to emotional health and clear thinking*, HG Publishing.

[5] See WHO website: http://www.who.int/mental_health/management/depression/definition/en/

[6] David O. Antonuccio and William G. Danton; Garland Y. DeNelsky, Psychotherapy Versus Medication for Depression: Challenging the Conventional Wisdom With Data, *Professional Psychology: Research and Practice*, December 1995 Vol. 26, No. 6, 574–585

[7] For a fuller understanding of depression, see http://www.clinical-depression.co.uk/learning_path.htm

37460815R00115

Made in the USA
Charleston, SC
11 January 2015